STANDARDS-BASED LEARNING FOR STUDENTS WITH DISABILITIES

Allan A. Glatthorn

Marsha Craft-Tripp

EYE ON EDUCATION
6 DEPOT WAY WEST, SUITE 106
LARCHMONT, NY 10538
(914) 833–0551
(914) 833–0761 fax
www.eyeoneducation.com

Library of Congress Cataloging-in-Publication Data

Glatthorn, Allan A., 1924–
    Standards-based learning for students with disabilities / by Allan A.
Glatthorn and Marsha Craft-Tripp.
    p. cm.
    ISBN 1-930556-01-2
    1. Handicapped children—Education—Standards—United States
I. Craft-Tripp, Marsha, 1952– II. Title.

LC3981.G52 2000
371.9—dc21

                                                            00-028778

10 9 8 7 6 5 4 3 2 1

Cover design and illustration by Carolyn H. Edlund
Editorial and production services provided by
Richard H. Adin Freelance Editorial Services
52 Oakwood Blvd., Poughkeepsie, NY 12603-4112
(914-471-3566)

Also Available from EYE ON EDUCATION

Self-Efficacy:
Raising the Bar for Students
With Learning Needs
by Joanne Eisenberger,
Marcia Conti-D'Antonio,
and Robert Bertrando

Making Decisions about Diverse Learners:
A Guide for Educators
by Fern Aefsky

Supporting Students with Learning
Needs in the Block
by Marcia Conti-D'Antonio,
Robert Bertrando,
and Joanne Eisenberger

Personalized Instruction:
Changing Classroom Practice
by James W. Keefe and John M. Jenkins

Coaching and Mentoring
First-Year and Student Teachers
by India J. Podsen and Vicki M. Denmark

Transforming Schools into
Community Learning Centers
by Steve R. Parson

The Directory of Programs
for Students At Risk
by Thomas L. Williams

MEET THE AUTHORS

Allan A. Glatthorn is Distinguished Research Professor of Education at East Carolina University, where he teaches courses in supervision and curriculum. His career in education spans several decades and roles. When a classroom teacher, he taught students with disabilities and gifted students. He is the author of numerous professional books, three of which have been published by Eye on Education.

Marsha Craft-Tripp is Director of Student Accountability for the Beaufort County (North Carolina) schools. A former teacher of students with disabilites, she also served as director and supervisor of special education for 27 years. She holds the Ph.D. degree from North Carolina State University.

ACKNOWLEDGMENTS

We acknowledge our indebtedness to all those researchers who have generated sound knowledge about students with disabilities and to all those educators who have served those students so well.

On a personal level, we are happy to acknowledge the special support we received from Bob Sickles, our publisher, who first saw the need for this work. And in the background, supporting and advising, were our very special spouses.

Allan Glatthorn
Marsha Craft-Tripp

TABLE OF CONTENTS

PREFACE

We write this book for all educators who work with students with disabilities. We confess that we hold high expectations for these students. We believe that they too can meet realistic standards that recognize both their strengths and limitations. The standards we have identified in this work should, however, not be viewed as inflexible hurdles for all students with disabilities. They should be seen instead as flexible guidelines to help teachers challenge students and establish quality programs. Neither should they be seen as final pronouncements. Instead they should be viewed as the best available knowledge at the time of this writing, subject to change as new knowledge is developed.

The book begins by building the knowledge base about the two central concepts: the nature of standards and the most common disabilities found in students in the classroom. Chapters 3, 4, and 5 examine what we term "the foundation elements"—the comprehensive learning environment in which the standards become operationalized. Chapter 3 develops the standards for the school culture, as a supportive culture is essential. Chapter 4 is intended to help teachers work together in establishing a learning community, one where students with disabilities feel needed and accepted. The final chapter in this foundational section examines both the opportunity standards and the constraints affecting teachers. The chapter is intended to provide balance in developing an educational program for these students. We note this irony: though there is much talk about curriculum standards and performance standards, there is very little discussion of opportunity standards—the opportunities students need if they are to meet the content and performance standards.

The middle section of the book comprises six chapters, each of which considers in depth the core elements of standards-based programs: curriculum, long-term plans, performance tasks, units of study, performance assessments, and instruction.

The final section of the book considers what we term the "facilitating components"—the IEP and the learning structures.

We should note here two issues of terminology. Though many educators use the term *standards* in a narrow sense of curriculum requirements, we use the term in a broader sense: a set of expectations for students, teachers, and administrators. Readers will also note that we use the term *grades* to refer to a placement level. We do so simply for the sake of clarity. We understand that the best programs for students with disabilities ignore rigid grade levels, developing instead individualized interventions that are needs based, not age based.

We hope the book makes it easier to develop quality programs for students with disabilities. Though the term *special* is no longer in current use in the profession, we consider these students as very special people and dedicate this book to them.

Allan A. Glatthorn
Marsha Craft-Tripp

PART I

SEEING THE
BIG PICTURE

1

UNDERSTANDING STANDARDS-BASED LEARNING

This book is about *standards-based learning* for students with disabilities. Rather than being simply a current "buzz word," the term denotes a specific approach for the learning of all students who have a range of disabilities. As a foundation for what follows, this chapter defines the concept and examines its implications. In accomplishing this goal, the chapter also serves as an organizer for the rest of the book.

UNDERSTANDING THE CONCEPT OF STANDARDS

The term *standards* is used in three different senses. *Curriculum standards* (sometimes called *content standards*) identify what students are to learn in one subject, K–12. Here is a curriculum or content standard: The student will learn money management skills, saving, and spending in a prudent manner. Curriculum standards for students with disabilities are explained in Chapter 6.

Performance standards state the quality of the performance considered satisfactory. Here is an example of a performance standard: The student will develop a weekly budget that meets three criteria: (a) allocates 20 percent of what is earned to savings; (b) shows a reasonable amount allocated to personal needs; and (c) stays within the limits of income. Chapter 10 discusses performance standards.

Opportunity standards identify the opportunities that students need if they are to accomplish the performance standards. Here are some of the opportunities that are needed by students with disabilities: a planned program; individualized instruction; grouping that does not stigmatize them; a responsive curriculum; and adequate time for learning. Chapter 5 explains opportunity standards.

These three types of standards are all included in standards-based learning, which is defined in this manner: Standards-based learning is learning whose content is clearly defined, that meets explicit levels of performance, and that requires sufficient opportunities for learning.

Figure 1.1 represents schematically the key aspects of standards-based learning. As the figure indicates, those aspects include the central goal, the foundation elements, the key attributes, and the facilitative components, each of which will be examined below.

THE CENTRAL GOAL

As Figure 1.1 suggests, at the center is standards-based learning for students with disabilities. All the other elements are intended to influence or contribute to this goal, either directly or indirectly. In essence, as the figure suggests, all that matters is results, construed broadly. For students with disabilities, the desired results include development of physical, mental, and emotional abilities. Achieving those results requires an understanding of the students, as explained in Chapter 2.

THE FOUNDATION ELEMENTS

Three elements provide a foundation for standards-based learning.

SCHOOL AND CLASSROOM CULTURE

For standards-based learning to operate effectively, it requires a supportive school environment. The chief aspect of the school and classroom environment is the culture. The term *culture* has been defined variously. (For a review of the different definitions, see Cunningham & Gresso, 1993.) The following definition has been derived from a review of that source and other literature: The values of a group of people who share a common place and purpose. These shared values result in norms, or similar ways of behaving, and are manifested in celebrations, ceremonies, customs, and other events.

FIGURE 1.1. STANDARDS-BASED LEARNING

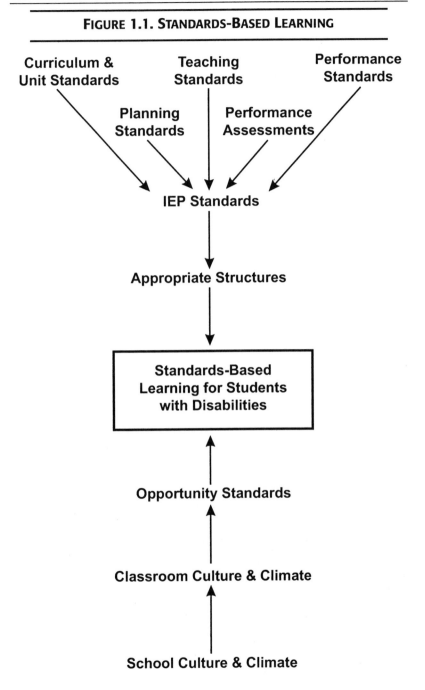

To understand the importance of culture, consider these examples. The faculty of School A share a belief that students with disabilities are problem students who need to be segregated from the rest of the student population. The faculty of School B, on the other hand, believe that students with disabilities are unique individuals who can learn best in the regular classroom. Evidently, those differing cultures will result in very different environments and procedures. Chapter 3 provides a more detailed analysis of cultural standards that support learning for all students with disabilities.

In an attempt to crystallize their school's culture, several faculties have developed written statements of their shared beliefs. An example of one such statement is shown in Figure 1.2. Faculties should keep in mind that the deeply held beliefs matter much more than such written statements.

FIGURE 1.2. BELIEFS OF THE FACULTY OF WASHINGTON MIDDLE SCHOOL

We Believe...

1. That learning is the goal for everyone: students, administrators, teachers, and parents. All that matters is results.

2. That all students can achieve, given the needed supports.

3. That all students have both talents and limitations.

4. That all students are individuals who are more than the labels we give them.

5. That all students learn most when they learn to accept themselves and each other. For most students that acceptance is best developed in inclusive environments.

6. That all parents should be actively involved in the education of their sons and daughters. This involvement is especially crucial for students with disabilities.

. 7. That the best results for all students are achieved through teamwork and collaboration. Such cooperation and teamwork are critically important for students with disabilities.

___

SCHOOL AND CLASSROOM CLIMATE

Climate is the emotional "weather" of the school and the classroom. A review of the literature suggests that the following attributes would best facilitate standards-based learning. (See, for example, McGregor & Vogelsberg, 1998.)

♦ Safe and secure

Students feel safe in the school, not anxious about their security. Students with disabilities believe that they will not be harmed.

♦ Clean and inviting

The physical environment is clean and well maintained. The school looks inviting, and teachers and administrators make the students feel welcome. Students with disabilities feel as if they belong.

♦ Warm and friendly

Students do not feel isolated and alone. Visitors are greeted in a friendly manner. Parents are welcomed. Students with disabilities are included, not excluded.

♦ Challenging and supportive

High expectations are held for administrators, teachers, and students. Students with disabilities are given the support they need to achieve those expectations.

A further discussion of the climate desired in a school that functions as a community of learners can be found in Chapter 4.

OPPORTUNITY STANDARDS

As noted above, opportunity standards are statements of the opportunities and supports that students need if they are to achieve what is expected of them. For example, it is manifestly unfair if students are expected to achieve at a satisfactory level if they do not have qualified teachers.

Several opportunity standards are especially important for students with disabilities. First, they need an opportunity to learn in inclusive classrooms where they are valued for what they are, not stigmatized by a label. They need teachers who accept them and know how to bring out the best in them. They must have the opportunity of mastering a challenging but appropriate curriculum. They need sufficient time to achieve what is expected of them. They deserve quality learning resources—computers, media, and print materials. These elements, as well as the constraints special educators face, are more fully explained in Chapter 5.

THE KEY ATTRIBUTES

Five key attributes impact directly on standards-based learning.

CURRICULUM STANDARDS

Curriculum standards, sometimes called *content standards*, specify what students are to learn. Chapter 6 discusses what is termed a *three-part curriculum*—the regular curriculum, the special curriculum, and the individual curriculum.

PLANNING STANDARDS

Long-term plans that provide a general time line for instruction facilitate the implementation of the IEP by charting the units to be taught. Although the student with a disability has an individualized program, a general plan is also helpful if the student with a disability is to be fully included in the regular class activities. This is discussed in Chapter 7.

PERFORMANCE TASKS AND UNITS

Chapter 9 describes in detail how to develop standards based units for students with disabilities. The centerpiece of standards based units is a *performance task*, a complex and open-ended problem that students are expected to solve.

PERFORMANCE ASSESSMENTS
AND STANDARDS

A performance assessment is an evaluation of the student's performance in completing the performance task. To assist both the teacher and the students in making valid assessments, the teacher develops *rubrics* that indicate clearly the performance standard.

Performance standards specify the level of performance considered satisfactory. To understand the term, consider this example from the world of sports. A college football coach who is recruiting high school students makes it clear that he wants a quarterback who has a pass completion rate of more than 60 percent. Sixty percent is the performance standard. A teacher testing students with disabilities on their skills in computation might specify that he or she expects students to get 7 of 10 problems correct. That is the performance standard. Performance standards for students with disabilities should be challenging but attainable with effort and assistance. Chapter 9 explains these matters more fully.

STANDARDS FOR
EFFECTIVE TEACHING

The most significant attribute is effective teaching. *Effective teaching* is defined here as "teaching that maximizes student learning." The emphasis is on student learning, not a specific teaching method, as explained in Chapter 11.

FACILITATIVE COMPONENTS

Two components facilitate the implementation of the key attributes.

INDIVIDUALIZED
EDUCATIONAL PROGRAM

The IEP is a means for systematizing the delivery of the key attributes. As such, it is only a means to an end, not an end to itself. However, it is a vitally important means for drawing together the standards-based curriculum, the student performance standard, and the opportunity standard. The IEP, discussed more fully in Chapter 12, is a blueprint for enabling the student with a disability to achieve standards-based learning.

APPROPRIATE STRUCTURES

The final facilitative component is the appropriate structures for learning. These structures can be identified by reflecting on and answering five questions:

1. Where will the student with a disability learn? Will he or she learn best in an inclusive classroom, in a resource room, in a special facility (such as a computer laboratory), or in a special school?

2. With whom will the student with a disability learn? Will he or she learn best by working alone, working with age mates of all types, or working with other students with disabilities?

3. What instructional assistance will be provided? Will the student with a disability be taught by the computer, by a peer, by the regular classroom teacher, by the special educator, or by a classroom aide?

4. In what size group will the student with a disability accomplish most? Should he or she be in a class-sized learning group, be part of a small group, or work independently?

5. How will planning time be provided to staff? Should the school adopt block scheduling or some other scheduling alternative that will provide for increased planning time? (See Zemelman, Daniels, & Hyde, 1998.)

How best to answer these questions for students with disabilities is discussed in Chapter 13.

A CONCLUDING NOTE

Some educators believe that the standards movement should proceed without involving students with disabilities. The view expressed here is that standards can significantly improve special education if those standards are used flexibly, sensitively, and meaningfully.

REFERENCES

Cunningham, W. C., & Gresso, D. W. (1993). *Cultural leadership.* Needham Heights, MA: Allyn & Bacon.

McGregor, G., & Vogelsberg, R. T. (1998). *Inclusive schooling practices: Pedagogical and research foundations.* Baltimore: Brookes.

Zemelman, S., Daniels, H., & Hyde, A. (1998). *Best practice* (2d ed.). Portsmouth, NH: Heinemann.

2

UNDERSTANDING STUDENTS WITH DISABILITIES

Some educators who do not understand special education hold damaging stereotypes about students with disabilities: "They are all slow learners and troubled kids." This stereotype interferes with students with disabilities being able to accomplish standards-based learning, because it obscures significant differences. This chapter provides the essential knowledge about students with disabilities, so that their teachers can help them accomplish standards-based learning. Twelve categories of students with disabilities are identified, with the four most common types explained in full.

THE GENERAL PICTURE

Prior to the implementation of the Individuals with Disabilities Education Act of 1975, approximately one million children with disabilities were shut out of school and hundreds of thousands more were denied appropriate educational services. During the 1993–94 school year approximately 12 percent of elementary and secondary students received special education services. Over 95 percent of these students received services in regular school buildings and many in regular classrooms. Many are learning and achieving at levels previously thought impossible. As a result they are graduating from high school, going to college, and entering the work force as productive citizens in unprecedented numbers (U.S. Department of Education, 1997).

To work effectively with students with disabilities, you need to understand who they are and how they learn. In accomplishing these goals, you will need to understand the categories of handicapping conditions. However, keep in mind that there is much dissatisfaction with the way that students with disabilities are classified. Reschly (1987) notes that the current system evolved "gradually, haphazardly, and inconsistently" over the past century (p. 37). And Ysseldyke (1998) points out that the classification decisions typically lack reliability. Despite these reservations, the categories continue to play in important role in the placement and intervention processes.

There are 12 categories typically used in classifying the disabled. The last two categories, autism and traumatic brain-injured, are new categories included in Congress's 1990 amendment.

+ Learning disabled
+ Speech or language impaired
+ Mentally disabled
+ Emotionally disabled
+ Multiple disabilities
+ Other health impaired (including ADHD)
+ Deaf or hearing impaired
+ Blind or visually impaired
+ Orthopedically impaired
+ Deaf and blind
+ Autistic
+ Traumatic brain-injured

The following discussion first examines the three categories of students commonly found in regular classrooms and then notes briefly the other less commonly found types of disabilities.

LEARNING DISABLED

The number of children classified as learning disabled has increased substantially over the last 20 years. In 1976, children identified with learning disabilities (LD) numbered 783,000. By 1992–93 this population exceeded 2.3 million. These children currently comprise almost half of all the placements into special education. Public schools spend approximately $8,000 a year to educate an LD student, compared to $5,500 for a nondisabled student. (U.S. Office of Education, 1996).

UNDERSTANDING LEARNING DISABILITY

Most studies published in psychological, educational, and neuropsychological journals define persons with a learning disability as those with at least average ability to process and retrieve some information from their environment, but who unexpectedly have difficulty performing at their age level on specific cognitive tasks. Their performance on intelligence tests is within the average range, but they exhibit problems in academic tasks. The definition of learning disabilities given in 1981 by the National Joint Commission for Learning Disabilities is as follows:

> Learning disabilities is a generic term that refers to a heterogeneous group of disorders manifested by significant difficulties in the acquisition and use of listening, speaking, reading, writing, reasoning, or mathematical abilities. These disorders are intrinsic to the individual and are presumed to be due to central nervous system dysfunction. Even though a learning disability may occur concomitantly with other handicapping conditions (e.g., sensory impairment, mental disability, social, or emotional disturbance) or environmental influences (e.g., cultural differences, insufficient/inappropriate instruction, psychogenic factors), it is not the direct result of these conditions or influences. (Hammill, Leigh, McNutt, & Larsen, 1981, p. 336.)

When attempting to classify children suspected of having a learning disability, a concerted effort should be made to establish that the disability is not a result of inadequate opportunity to learn. Learning disability is not the result of inadequate teaching or lack of exposure to concepts but rather to basic disorders in psychological processes (Spafford & Grosser, 1996).

HELPING THE LEARNING DISABLED

In general the research has determined that students with learning disabilities profit most from the following strategies:

- Teaching the standard curriculum with adaptations, including content and learning methods.
- Using cooperative learning groups, usually of a heterogeneous nature, with assistance from other group members.
- Using project-based learning. Students work together on a complex project, with students choosing the way they will learn.
- Teaching specific learning strategy. A learning strategy is a mental process that simplifies the learning process. For example, using a tree diagram as a means of showing relationships is a learning strategy.

EMOTIONALLY DISABLED

Definitions of emotionally disabled usually include references to such emotional features as frequency, chronicity, arousal level, situation, age-appropriateness, and coping ability. There is no single demarcation on the continuum from normal to abnormal. There is no single definition of a behavioral disorder; therefore the definition is subjective (Kaufman, 1981).

UNDERSTANDING THE EMOTIONALLY DISABLED

As defined in the Individual with Disabilities Education Act, those who are emotionally disabled exhibit one or more of the following characteristics over a long period of time and to a marked degree:

- It is an inability to learn that cannot be explained by intellectual, sensory, or health factors.
- It is characterized by an inability to build or maintain satisfactory interpersonal relationships with peers or teachers.
- The child exhibits inappropriate types of behavior or feelings under normal circumstances.

- ♦ A general mood of unhappiness or depression is present.
- ♦ There is a tendency to develop physical symptoms or fears associated with personal or school problems.

The term does not apply to children who are socially maladjusted unless it is determined that they have an emotional disturbance (Individuals with Disabilities Education Act [IDEA], 1997).

For years the U.S. Department of Education estimated that 2 percent of the school-age population were seriously emotionally disabled; however, in 1993 frequency was estimated as less than 1 percent. Despite this low frequency, it is reasonable to assume that every teacher has had contact with students whose stress causes varying degrees of academic and/or social frustration. The responses of these students often cause conflict with their teachers, other authority figures, and peers. Sometimes their behaviors are so severe that the educational process is disrupted (Gallagher, 1995). Such students may be characterized by low self-esteem, poor impulse control, defiance of authority figures, minimal social interaction skills, conduct disorders, personality disorders, problems in getting along with others, personal struggle with controlling self, aggressive behaviors, insecurities, and withdrawn nature (Shinsky, 1997).

HELPING THE EMOTIONALLY DISABLED

Services for the emotionally disabled fall into a continuum of instructional arrangements designed to accommodate the child's individual needs. Some educators believe that the least restrictive environment is the regular classroom, while others believe that the least restrictive environment is the placement that provides the right amount of structure for the child (Gallagher, 1995). Regardless of the setting, those with emotional problems can profit from the right kind of environment and appropriate intervention strategies.

The appropriate environment will vary with the individual, of course. However, many of those who teach students who are emotionally disabled report that those students learn best in a classroom that is structured, predictable, and stable. These students need help with their social skills to help them learn self-control. Self-control can be taught by using such strategies as coaching, modeling, and teaching students how to teach themselves (Elliott & Graham, 1991).

ATTENTION DEFICIT DISORDER

Attention deficit disorder (ADD) is often classified under the category of "other health impaired" and is recognized as a handicapping condition. (The condition is also termed ADHD, attention deficit hyperactivity disorder.) A child may receive services as would an other health impaired student if the ADD is determined to be a chronic health problem that results in limited alertness, that adversely affects educational performance, and that requires special education services. There have been many court decisions requiring school systems to provide special services to ADD children. An informal policy letter issued by the U.S. Department of Education in October, 1991 informed school systems that they are required to provide special education services to students with ADD (Cohen, 1996).

Once called *hyperkinesis* or *minimal brain dysfunction*, ADD is one of the most common mental disorders among children. It affects 3 to 5 percent of all children. On the average, at least one child in every classroom in America needs help for this disorder. It can lead to a lifetime of frustrated dreams—as well as ongoing frustration for the family (Gordon & Asher, 1994).

DEFINITION OF ATTENTION DEFICIT DISORDER

Attention deficit disorder is a developmental disorder of self-control, consisting of problems with attention span, impulse control, and activity level. It can be manifested with or without hyperactivity. It is usually present before the age of seven, although many individuals are diagnosed after the symptoms have been present for a number of years (Shinsky, 1996).

MAJOR CHARACTERISTICS OF
ATTENTION DEFICIT DISORDER

The characteristics of attention deficit disorder fall into three general areas: difficulty sustaining attention, difficulty controlling impulses, and problems with too much behavior (McBurnett, Lahey, & Pfiffner, 1993; Shinsky, 1996). Each of these three areas is discussed below.

DIFFICULTY SUSTAINING ATTENTION

Research shows that students with ADD have trouble sustaining their attention to activities for long periods of time, especially those that are boring, repetitive, or tedious. They cannot persist in their efforts to concentrate and find themselves drawn away by anything that may be stimulating or interesting. Students with ADD get bored or lose interest in their work much faster than those without ADD. They seem to be drawn to the most rewarding or reinforcing aspects of any situation.

Children with ADD have a problem with deferred gratification. They choose doing a little work now for a small immediate reward, rather than doing more work now for a bigger reward later. Those with ADD are less prepared for the future. They often go from crisis to crisis not prepared for an upcoming event or assignment. They have an altered sense of time. Most things take longer than what they expect. Appointments and missed deadlines can lead to others' perception of them as unreliable (Fowler, 1994; Shinsky, 1996).

DIFFICULTY CONTROLLING IMPULSES

Children with ADD have trouble waiting. *Now* is the key word. They have a decreased ability to inhibit behavior or control impulses control. They do not think before they act or speak and speak loudly and excessively. They blurt out comments they have not thought about before speaking. They start assignments without reading the directions carefully and want to be the first one finished whether the assignment is correct or not.

Children with ADD take shortcuts. They put forth the least amount of effort and take the least amount of time to perform boring or unpleasant tasks. They take too many risks. Their impulsiveness may also show up in greater risk taking. They may be more accident prone because they do not think about consequences.

Those with ADD also have money management problems, because of their impulsiveness. Before spending money, they do not think about the consequences to their budgets.

Children with ADD have problems with impulsive thinking as well as impulsive behavior. They find it harder to keep their minds on their work and to inhibit thoughts not related to the task at hand. Often they have difficulty in maintaining a conversation because their minds wander. They are also more emotional than others. They do not inhibit their first reactions to a situation, not taking time to separate their feelings from the facts. Children with ADD do not analyze tasks into many parts, thus damaging their problem-solving skills (Fowler, 1994; Shinsky, 1996).

A PROBLEM WITH
TOO MUCH BEHAVIOR

Children with ADD may be hyperactive. This appears as restlessness, fidgeting, pacing, and excessive moving or talking. They do not regulate or manage their activity level to meet the demands of the moment (American Psychiatric Association, 1994).

Children with ADD may also be hyperresponsive. They are more likely than others to respond to things around them in any situation. They are not inhibited. Their behavior occurs too quickly and too frequently. This means that the hyperactivity and the impulsiveness are part of the same underlying problem of inhibiting behavior. They have difficulty returning to their work once their attention is broken.

Children with ADD have difficulty following through on instructions and following the rules. They often engage in activities unrelated to what they were told to do. Because of this, most people view them as lazy and unmotivated. Those with ADD do not exhibit self-speech as others do. Self-speech is the language that guides and govern behaviors. This ineffective self-speech hinders them further in their impulse control, self-control, and the use of plans to guide their behavior.

Children with ADD work inconsistently. They are capable of producing acceptable work. At times they are able to complete their work easily; at other times they do not complete their work. The problem is that they cannot maintain this consistent pattern of work productivity the way others can. They are influenced more by the moment than by a thought-out plan or rule (Barkley, 1995).

USING EFFECTIVE STRATEGIES

In working with ADD children and youth, educators should find that the following teaching/learning strategies would be most effective. First, these students can profit from a behavior management system that uses sensitively an appropriate reward system for productive learning behaviors. They also profit from a curriculum that helps them develop such organizational skills as short- and long-term planning and time management. Teachers can also help them manage their learning by using such strategies as organizing a notebook, taking good notes, scheduling homework time, and preparing for tests.

MENTALLY DISABLED

Students who are mentally disabled fall into one of three categories: the mildly (educable), moderately (trainable), or severely (profound) retarded. Students who fall under the mild category generally score between 50 and 70 on an individually administered intelligence test. Students who fall within the moderate range generally score between 25 and 49; severe/profound students fall below 25. Most classroom teachers work with the mildly retarded students.

UNDERSTANDING THE MENTALLY DISABLED

Students who qualify for special education services in the area of educable mentally disabled demonstrate significantly subaverage general intellectual functioning that exists concurrently with deficits in adaptive behavior. These deficits are usually manifested during the developmental period, adversely affecting their educational performance. They experience a lack of development in the cognitive domain. They can be taught useful reading, math skills, social skills, and self-help skills but skills must be taught in small, repetitive steps. Retention of information taught may be brief. These students are not emotionally disabled but may be immature. The information that they learn in one setting may not be applied to another setting. Change in routine may be difficult for these students; they may have trouble articulating needs and wants (Shinsky, 1997).

USING EFFECTIVE STRATEGIES

Three strategies seem effective in working with the mentally retarded. First, teachers should give these students additional time for learning tasks and slow their own pace of instruction. Teachers can also help by organizing the curriculum into smaller chunks, with more frequent assessment and feedback. Finally these students will need special help in learning the social and occupational skills that they will need in securing and retaining employment (Loyd & Brolin, 1997).

LESS COMMON DISABILITIES

Several disabilities are present among many children but are less commonly found in the regular classroom.

MULTIPLE DISABILITIES

Those with multiple disabilities exhibit more than one disability. A child may be mentally disabled and blind or autistic and orthopedically impaired. The combination of disabilities causes severe educational problems that require special educational services to meet each area of disability (IDEA, 1997).

OTHER HEALTH IMPAIRED

A child with an "other health impairment" has limited strength, vitality, or alertness because of a chronic or acute health problem. It may be a heart condition; tuberculosis; rheumatic fever; nephritis; asthma; sickle-cell anemia; hemophilia; epilepsy; lead poisoning; leukemia; diabetes; or an attention deficit disorder. The presence of the health problem adversely affects a child's educational performance (IDEA, 1997). The majority of the children identified as "other health impaired" have an attention deficit disorder, as explained above.

SPEECH OR LANGUAGE IMPAIRED

Speech impaired children have a communication disorder, such as problems with fluency, problems with articulation or voice, or a language impairment. All of these adversely affect a child's educational performance (Shinsky, 1996).

♦ Fluency disorders

A fluency disorder is an interruption in the flow or rhythm of speech. It can be characterized by hesitations, repetitions, or prolongations of a sound, syllable, word, or phrase. Stuttering is one type of fluency problem (Gearheart & Weishahn, 1980).

♦ Articulation disorders

A child with an articulation disorder has difficulties with the way sounds are formed and strung together. It can be characterized by substituting one sound for another, omitting a sound or distorting a sound (Gearheart & Weishahn, 1980).

♦ Voice disorders

Voice disorders include problems with pitch, loudness, or quality. Pitch problems (too high or too low) seldom cause any serious difficulty to the speaker. Voice intensity (too loud or too soft) is often not a problem in itself but could indicate a hearing problem. Voice quality is the most common voice disorder. Voice quality can be a problem of breathiness, harshness, and nasality. It can also be a flexibility disorder such as speaking in a monotone voice (Gearheart & Weishahn, 1980).

♦ Language disorders

Language disorders are the most difficult disorders of speech to diagnose with certainty. Those disorders are characterized by a marked slowness in the onset and development of language skills necessary for expressing ideas and for understanding the ideas that a child reads or hears (Gearheart & Weis-hahn, 1980).

DEAF OR HEARING IMPAIRED

Students with hearing impairments demonstrate a hearing loss which interferes with their development or adversely affects educational performance in the regular classroom. Their hearing loss can range from mild to severe deafness. Their hearing loss causes language and communication deficits. Students may wear hearing aids for amplification or may require the use of an auditory trainer. Deaf students will rely on sign language or some alternative mode of communication. It is important that preferential seating and proper lighting be provided to these children, as well as maintaining good eye contact and using distinct lip movements when speaking (Shinsky, 1996).

BLIND OR VISUALLY IMPAIRED

The visually impaired classification includes children who are blind or who have an impairment in their vision that, even with correction, adversely affects a child's educational performance. They require educational modifications and adaptations. Their needs may range from the use of large-print textbooks to the use of Braille or taped materials. In addition, the ability of a visually impaired student to move about independently may be impaired. If so, the student would need training in orientation and mobility. Orientation is the ability to use one's remaining senses to establish his or her position in relationship to objects in the environment. Mobility is the ability to move from one location to another (Gearheart & Weishahn, 1986).

ORTHOPEDICALLY IMPAIRED

Children with orthopedic impairments have an impairment caused by a congenital problem such as being born with a club foot or missing an arm or leg. It can also be an impairment caused by a disease such as polio or a result of other causes such as cerebral palsy or amputations. Whatever the cause, the impairment must affect a child's educational performance and require special education services or special accommodations (IDEA, 1997).

DEAF AND BLIND

This is a combined disability of blindness and deafness. The combination of these two disabilities causes such severe problems that these children cannot be accommodated in specialized programs solely for the blind or the deaf (IDEA, 1997).

AUTISTIC

According to the federal regulations (Section 300.7), autism is a developmental disability that significantly affects verbal and nonverbal communication and social interaction. Its onset is generally before the age of three and adversely affects a child's educational performance. Autistic children often engage in repetitive activities and stereotyped movements. These children are very resistant to changes in their routine or in their environment. About 50 percent of autistic children are nonverbal. Autism is a lifelong disability that makes learning difficult and can lead to serious behavior problems (Shinsky, 1996).

TRAUMATIC BRAIN-INJURED

A traumatic brain injury is an acquired injury to the brain caused by an external physical force, resulting in total or partial functional disability or psychosocial impairment or both. It can affect a child's ability to function cognitively, socially, or physically. Some of the areas that can be affected are language, memory, attention, reasoning, judgment, abstract reasoning, problem solving, behavior, informational processing, or speech (IDEA, 1997). Students with a traumatic brain injury may experience high frustration levels, irritability, and fatigue. In school they may experience difficulty in learning new information, recalling events from earlier in the day, and focusing attention. They may not be able to understand abstract meanings, such as figures of speech, or to consider a variety of possible solutions (Shinsky, 1996).

A CONCLUDING NOTE

This chapter provided an overview of the categories of special needs learners along with characteristics of these children. Keep in mind that these categories and labels are only generalizations that obscure the uniqueness of each student classified as *special*.

REFERENCES

American Psychiatric Association. (1994). *Diagnostic and statistical manual of mental disorders* (4th ed.). Washington, DC: Author.

Barkley, R. A. (1995). *Taking charge of ADHD*. New York: Guilford Press.

Cohen, M. D. (1996). Summary of IDEA/Section 504. In CH.A. D.D. (Eds.), *ADD and adolescents* (pp. 52–62). Plantation, FL: Children and Adults with Attention Deficit Disorder.

Elliott, S. N., & Gresham, F. M. (1991). *Social skills intervention guide*. Circle Pines, MN: American Guidance Service.

Fowler, M. (1994). *Attention-deficit hyperactivity disorder*. Washington, DC: National Information Center for Children and Youth with Disabilities.

Gallagher, P. A. (1995). *Teaching students with behavior disorders: Techniques and activities for classroom instruction*. Denver, CO: Love.

Gearheart, B. R., & Weishahn, M. W. (1980). *The handicapped student in the regular classroom*. St. Louis, MO: Mosby.

Gordon, S. B., & Asher, M. J. (1994). *Meeting the ADD challenge: A practical guide for teachers*. Champaign, IL: Research Press.

Hammill, D. D., Leigh, J. E., McNutt, G., & Larsen, S. C. (1981). A new definition of learning disabilities. *Learning Disability Quarterly, 4*, 336–42.

Individuals With Disabilities Education Act, 34 C.F.R. part 300 (1997).

Kauffman, J. (1981). *Characteristics of children's behavior disorders* (2nd ed.). Columbus, OH: Charles E. Merrill.

Loyd, R. J., & Brolin, D. E. (1997). *Life centered education*. Reston, VA: Council for Exceptional Children.

McBurnett, K., Lahey, B. B., & Pfiffner, L. J. (1993). Diagnosis of attention deficit disorders in DSM-IV: Scientific basis and implications for education. *Exceptional Children, 60*, 108–117.

Reschly, D. J. (1987). Learning characteristics of mildly handicapped students. In M. C. Wang, M. C. Reynolds, & H. J. Walberg (eds.), *Handbook of special education: Research and practice: Volume 1, Learner characteristics and adaptive education* (pp. 35–58). New York: Pergamon.

Shinsky, E. J. (1996). *Students with special needs: A resource guide for teachers.* Lansing, MI: Shinsky Seminars.

Shinsky, E. J. (1997). *Techniques for including students with disabilities.* Lansing, MI: Shinsky Seminars, Inc.

Spafford, C. S., & Grosser, G. S. (1996). *Dyslexia: Research and resource guide.* Boston: Allyn & Bacon.

U.S. Department of Education. (1996). Number and disabilities of children and youth served under IDEA, Part B. www.ed.gov/pubs/OSEP96AnlRpt/chap1b.html.

U.S. Department of Education. (1997). IDEA 1997: General information. www.ed.gov/offices/OSERS/IDEA/overview.html.

Ysseldyke, J. E. (1987). Classification of handicapped students. In M. C. Wang, M. C. Reynolds, & H. J. Walberg (eds.), *Handbook of special education: Research and practice: Volume 1, Learner characteristics and adaptive education* (pp. 253–272). New York: Pergamon.

PART II

THE FOUNDATION ELEMENTS

3

DEVELOPING A SCHOOL CULTURE THAT MEETS THE STANDARDS

A standards-based curriculum and standards-based teaching need a supportive organization if they are to flourish. As explained in Chapter 1, two of the most important aspects of the school organization are its culture and climate, which in turn affect the hidden curriculum. This chapter explains these concepts and identify the standards that schools should meet in these areas.

Understanding the Concept of Culture and Its Related Elements

The *culture* of a school, as explained in Chapter 1, is broadly construed as the interactions of three related elements—the core values, the norms of behavior, and the surface manifestations.

The Core Values

As Figure 3.1 indicates, the core values of the organization's members constitute the foundation of the school's culture. Thus, some school faculties place great value on orderliness, promptness, and obedience. Others place greater value on the joy of learning in a more relaxed atmosphere.

FIGURE 3.1. CULTURE AND ITS RELATED ELEMENTS

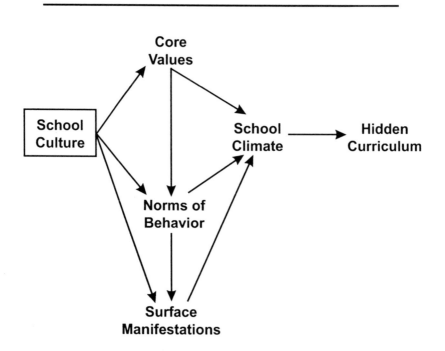

What values seem paramount if the culture is to support the learning of students with disabilities? The list offered in Figure 3.2 (p. 40), derived from a review of the literature, is offered as a set of faculty beliefs that can be used in faculty discussions and workshops. (See, for example, Bolman & Deal, 1991; Schein, 1991; and Cunningham & Gresso, 1993.) In the following paragraphs, we describe these values in fuller detail, and give some examples of their practical consequences.

- ◆ Learning is central for everyone

   This is perhaps the most essential of all. The message is communicated to all students and reinforced for students with disabilities. Teachers and administrators are also expected to learn—from the literature, from their experience, and from their reflective practice.

- All students can achieve at standard

  If standards are set so that they are challenging but attainable, and if students have the necessary opportunities, then even students with disabilities can achieve at the expected level. Simply setting standards is not enough. The students need effective teaching, a meaningful curriculum, and the time and materials required.

- All students have talents and limitations

  In this sense, all students are "special" and multidimensional. However, teachers should feel a significant responsibility to bring out the talents of students with disabilities. For example, many mildly disabled students are talented in the visual arts, in music, and in sports.

- All students are individuals

  This has been repeated so often that it has become a cliche. Leaders must help teachers get beyond the trite words and recognize the importance of seeing students as unique individuals. Labels such as *learning disabled* and *attention deficit disorder* obscure the individuality of students with disabilities.

- Accepting and valuing self and others are desirable for all students

  Accepting and valuing the self and others is essentially an attitude of "I'm OK, you're OK." In accepting and valuing the self, the individual understands what can be changed and what cannot be changed about the self—and acts accordingly. Such an attitude is a productive one, particularly for students with disabilities.

- Significant growth is best fostered by those who enact an attitude of inclusion

  The wording of this value is intended to emphasize an attitude and a belief system that result in the most supportive environment for each student. It is

FIGURE 3.2. STANDARDS FOR THE CULTURE

The following standards describe the expectations for a school culture that supports standards-based learning for students with disabilities:

- Core Values

  The faculty support the following values:

  1. Learning is central for everyone.
  2. All students can achieve at the expected standards, if they have the needed opportunities.
  3. All students have talents and limitations.
  4. All students are individuals who transcend the labels given them.
  5. Accepting and valuing self and others are desirable for all students.
  6. Significant growth is best fostered by those who enact an attitude of inclusiveness.
  7. All parents should be involved in the education of their children.
  8. For all students cooperation and collaboration are essential for maximum growth.

- Norms of Behavior

  The faculty endorse and operationalize the following norms of behavior, as they affect students with disabilities:

  1. We provide a quality standards-based curriculum for students with disabilities.
  2. We provide quality teaching for students with disabilities.
  3. We show respect for students with disabilities.
  4. We honor the special talents and accept the limitations of students with disabilities.
  5. We provide students with disabilities with all the time they need for maximum learning.

6. We involve the parents of students with disabilities in the education of their sons and daughters.

7. We provide for students with disabilities a supportive and inclusive learning environment.

8. We reward cooperation and collaboration.

- Surface Manifestations

The faculty endorse the following ways of demonstrating our culture as it affects students with disabilities:

1. We celebrate their achievements.

2. We recognize and reward their unique accomplishments.

3. We tell stories of heroes who excelled in spite of their limitations.

---

based, of course, on substantial research that indicates that including students with disabilities in the regular classroom has major benefits for all those involved. For students with disabilities, it has positive affective and cognitive outcomes. Students who are developing in the typical manner are benefitted from their involvement with students with disabilities. Though teachers are initially reluctant to adopt inclusive strategies, they become more confident about their ability to succeed as they gain more experience. (For an excellent synthesis of this literature, see McGregor and Vogelsberg, 1998.) That support for an attitude and behavior of inclusion should not be equated with an insistence that inclusion is best for everyone, however. Some students with disabilities will do better at certain ages in the resource room; some will need a special school.

- All parents should be involved in the education of their children

  The research provides strong support for the active involvement of all parents. Such meaningful involvement is one of the correlates of effective schools. (See Cotton, 1995.) It carries significant weight in the education of students with disabilities. And the attitude of faculty and administrators should be one of welcoming parents as partners in the education of their sons and daughters, rather than seeing parents as a nuisance to be tolerated because the law requires their involvement.

- For all students cooperation and collaboration are essential for maximum growth

  Cooperation and collaboration are powerful factors in the learning process. They are so essential that principals should model cooperation by working with teachers, teachers should work with each other, parents should collaborate, and students should work together in the learning process. Students with disabilities find the benefits particular advantageous, especially if they can contribute to the group. (See Johnson & Johnson, 1991; Kohn, 1992; and Slavin, 1990.)

THE NORMS OF BEHAVIOR

The norms of behavior grow out of the core values. Those norms represent "the way we do things around here." Thus in some schools the norm for teachers' leaving the school is "five minutes after students leave." In other schools, the norm is "one hour after the buses leave." One function of the mentors who work with new teachers is to inform the novices about the norms, since those norms are informal and typically not written. In too many schools the norm for treating students with disabilities is, "They can't learn so put them in the resource room." In other schools the norm is, " They can learn—so include them in everything you can."

The norms listed in Figure 3.2 (p. 40) are presented here as a set of standardized behaviors that emanate from the core values. They represent the core values as those values are operationalized in working with students with disabilities. Though they should not be imposed by the principal, strong leadership is needed to help teachers see the connection between their values and the norms of behavior. Open discussions are needed in which faculty have an opportunity to examine the norms, understand their implications, modify them as they wish, and then adopt them as self-imposed guidelines.

THE SURFACE MANIFESTATIONS

The surface manifestations also are a part of the culture; in fact, they are the part of the culture that most people understand. They include several activities that show what the culture looks like on the surface: the ceremonies and celebrations, such as assemblies that recognize the achievements of students with disabilities; the heroes, such as a fabled principal who years ago rejuvenated the school; the stories that old-timers tell about the good old days; and the rituals, such as saluting the flag every morning. Some educators writing about culture argue that these surface elements constitute the culture. The point here is that the core values are the primary components. The surface manifestations, such as those listed in Figure 3.2 (p. 40), are only the values in operation.

UNDERSTANDING SCHOOL CLIMATE

School climate is the "emotional weather" of a school, usually described with such terms as *warm, cold, friendly, unfriendly*. As Figure 3.1 (p. 38) indicates, the climate is affected by and grows out of the several aspects of culture.

The evidence suggests that students with disabilities flourish best in a special climate. The standards for that special climate include the following five elements:

1. *The physical environment* is inviting and safe. Classroom and other spaces are attractive and support learning. Students feel safe and secure.

2. *Interpersonal relationships* are appropriately informal and friendly, without being unprofessional and intrusive. For example, teachers take a personal interest in students with disabilities, without prying into their private affairs.

3. *Communications processes* are personal and individual. Administrators and teachers usually communicate with students with disabilities in a face-to-face manner.

4. *The task focus* is primarily on learning. Though relationships are important, they do not displace the learning priority.

5. *The goal structure* is cooperative, with competition used only selectively. For students with disabilities, cooperation is essential.

ANALYZING AND MODIFYING THE HIDDEN CURRICULUM

As suggested in Figure 3.1 (p. 38), culture and climate impact on the hidden curriculum for students with disabilities. The *hidden curriculum* is best defined in this manner: "What students learn from the culture, policies, and practices of the school." Such a curriculum is hidden because most administrators and teachers are unaware of it. Consider this example. The resource room is in a trailer that looks badly maintained. The principal visits the trailer once a year. The remoteness of the trailer, the separation from the main building, the poor maintenance, and the lack of administrative visiting are all part of that school's hidden curriculum. The message is clear: special education does not matter here.

The following process for analyzing the hidden curriculum for students with disabilities can be used by any faculty concerned with the hidden curriculum. First, a small task force should be appointed to plan and complete the task. The task force should include representatives of these constituencies: parents, classroom teachers, special education staff, district supervisors, and school administrators. The task force should design a study, determining which methods will be used. The simplest method would be to develop a survey based on the items noted in Figure 3.3 (p. 46), as revised by the task force. Figure 3.3 shows how the items could be used in a survey to determine the perceptions of the several groups.

The task force can then tally the responses of each group, assigning weights as follows: strongly agree, 1; agree, 2; disagree, 3; strongly disagree, 4. An "uncertain" response should be ignored in the tallying. In that manner, the items with the highest scores represent the most serious problems with the hidden curriculum. The task force can then decide how to modify those aspects that seem most serious. For example, if the survey indicates a problem with the language of respect, the principal could lead a discussion with the faculty on such topics as the importance of showing respect to and for students with disabilities; how words show respect; how body language shows respect.

A CONCLUDING NOTE

Teacher supervision tries to improve teaching, one teacher at a time. Cultural change, with its accompanying elements, can change an entire faculty.

FIGURE 3.3. EXAMINING THE HIDDEN CURRICULUM FOR STUDENTS WITH DISABILITIES

Your role (check one): Parent ___ Classroom teacher ___ Special education staff ___

To respondents: To helps us understand how certain practices might be affecting our students with disabilities, please complete the following survey. Consider each statement. Then circle your response, as follows:

SA: strongly agree

A: agree

D: disagree

SD: strongly disagree

?: uncertain

- Allocation of Resources
    1. The school district's budget provides adequately for the needs of students with disabilities.

        SA   A   D   SD   ?
    2. The school allocates sufficient time to the education of students with disabilities.

        SA   A   D   SD   ?
    3. The classroom space for students with disabilities is comparable in quality to that provided for regular students.

        SA   A   D   SD   ?
- Teaching
    1. The teachers who are assigned students with disabilities to their classrooms are as experienced and as effective as the rest of the faculty.

        SA   A   D   SD   ?
    2. All teachers receive effective training in fostering the achievement of students with disabilities.

        SA   A   D   SD   ?

3. Teachers assigned to students with disabilities are included in all significant school-based committees.

    SA   A   D   SD   ?

♦ Activity Program

1. Sponsors of activity programs encourage the participation of and welcome students with disabilities.

    SA   A   D   SD   ?

2. Special activity programs are offered that capitalize on the talents of students with disabilities.

    SA   A   D   SD   ?

♦ Communication

1. Students, teachers, and administrators use verbal and nonverbal language that connotes respect in talking to or about students with disabilities.

    SA   A   D   SD   ?

2. The communication of students, teachers, and administrators suggests that they can see beyond the labels and perceive the individuality of students with disabilities.

    SA   A   D   SD   ?

♦ Curriculum and Grouping

1. Students with disabilities have access to a quality curriculum.

    SA   A   D   SD   ?

2. Wherever feasible, students with disabilities are included in the regular classroom setting.

    SA   A   D   SD   ?

REFERENCES

Bolman, L. G., & Deal, T. E. (1991). *Reframing organizations.* San Francisco: Jossey-Bass.

Cotton, K. (1995). *Effective schooling practices: A research synthesis: 1995 update.* Portland, OR: Northwest Regional Educational Laboratory.

Cunningham, W. G., & Gresso, D. W. (1993). *Cultural leadership.* Needham Heights, MA: Allyn & Bacon.

Johnson, D. W., & Johnson, R. T. (1991). *Learning together and alone* (3rd ed.). Englewood Cliffs, NJ: Prentice Hall.

Kohn, A. (1992). *No contest: The case against competition.* New York: Houghton Mifflin.

McGregor, G., & Vogelsberg, R. T. (1998). *Inclusive schooling practices: Pedagogical and research foundations.* Baltimore, MD: Brookes.

Schein, E. H. (1991). *Organizational culture and leadership.* San Francisco: Jossey-Bass.

Slavin, R. E. (1990). *Cooperative learning.* Englewood Cliffs, NJ: Prentice Hall.

4

DEVELOPING A STANDARDS-BASED LEARNING COMMUNITY

As explained in the preceding chapter, the school can provide a supportive environment for all students. The individual classroom is even more important. The goal here is to make the classroom a *learning community.*

UNDERSTANDING THE NATURE
OF A LEARNING COMMUNITY

A *learning community*, as the term is used here, is a group of people who come together to learn, who feel responsible for each other, and who work together to accomplish shared goals. Sergiovanni (1994) summed it up this way: "Community can help teachers and students be transformed from a collection of 'I's' to a collective 'we'…" (p. xiii). Because each school and each classroom are different in significant ways, it is very difficult and perhaps unwise to suggest a general strategy for achieving community. However, the research and expert recommendations can provide some useful guidelines. (See, especially, Apple & Beane, 1995; McGregor & Vogelsberg, 1998.) The general guidelines are shown in Figure 4.1 and explained below.

FIGURE 4.1. CHARACTERISTICS OF A LEARNING COMMUNITY FOR STUDENTS WITH DISABILITIES

In a learning community, students demonstrate the following dispositions and behaviors:

- Demonstrate a sense of belonging.
- Show that they care for each other.
- Act responsibly.
- Show an appreciation of similarities and differences.
- Collaborate in the learning process.
- Experience a curriculum of community.
- Learn in an inviting environment.
- Use their power to affect their education.

BELONGING

It all begins with belonging, particularly for students with disabilities. When students feel that they belong, they speak of "our class," "our teacher," and "our room." They feel that they are part of a group, not an outsider. They believe that they are needed and that their absence will be noted when they miss class. Students with disabilities need this sense of belonging, because unfortunately they often feel ostracized and unwelcome.

Read how Walter, a mildly mentally disabled student, expresses his feelings of belonging:

> I like going to social studies. All the other kids help me learn. They don't tease me or call me names. I have my own desk. Mister Thompson always tells me that the class needs me.

Contrast that with how Jeannie, another student with a mild disability, sees her science class:

> I wish I didn't have to go to science. In the lab I just feel that I get in the way. There is nothing that I can do

there. Some of the kids tease me. Miss Cramer tries to stop them but they still do it.

Obviously those very different feelings would affect their motivation to learn.

In developing a classroom climate of belonging, the teaching team can make the greatest difference. Such behaviors as the following will produce positive results in this domain for the student with a disability:

- ◆ Calling on the students with disabilities. In general it makes sense to call on them when you believe that they can answer the question.

- ◆ Giving students with disabilities their own space. That special place should not be in the back or extreme sides of the room.

- ◆ Communicating with them frequently and warmly. All school personnel should learn and use first names in speaking to students with disabilities.

- ◆ Assigning appropriate tasks to students with disabilities. Be careful, however, that you do not turn them into "gofers" by giving them only menial tasks.

- ◆ Making sure that all students understand that exclusiveness will not be tolerated. Without embarrassing students with disabilities by referring to them specifically, help all the students understand that everyone needs to feel this sense of belonging. This is how one teacher expressed it to an inclusive class:

  > We don't have outsiders here. We all belong. We need everybody. Don't make anyone feel as if they don't belong here.

CARING

Because *caring* is one of those terms used loosely and understood vaguely, it would be useful to explain how a teacher expresses a feeling of caring for students with disabilities. First, the teacher should take a personal interest in the student with a disability: "Susan, how is your doll collection coming along?" Also the teacher should comment on the absence of a student with a disability. "We missed you yesterday, Jan. Were you not feeling well?" This personal caring should never be expressed so that it becomes an invasion of the student's privacy.

One who cares helps in a sensitive manner. Insensitive people do not understand that helping another often implies, "I don't think you can do it by yourself." To put it briefly, be helpful without being patronizing. To accomplish this goal, give help equally to all who need it, not just to students with disabilities.

Some teachers foolishly believe that caring involves accepting and praising whatever students offer. This "academic babying" seems to be especially common when teachers work with minority students and those with learning problems. Such behaviors communicate this negative message: "I think so little of you that I will praise whatever you do." Such comments to students with low ability undermine the teacher's credibility and confuse the slow learners, who see through this stratagem (Good & Brophy, 1997).

Students with disabilities also need how to learn to show caring to each other and the rest of the students. Many teachers have observed that mildly disabled students often tease each other; because they have not learned how to care for each other.

ACTING RESPONSIBLY

In the classroom community, all students act responsibly. This trait is manifested in two ways. The first is being able to control one's behavior. The several programs that attempt to help students control their own behavior differ in their approach but tend to teach the same skills. (See Good & Brophy, 1997.) These skills include:

- ♦ Understand what appropriate behavior is in school, at work, and in the neighborhood.
- ♦ Understand the consequences of inappropriate behavior.
- ♦ Monitor one's own behavior.

- Know how to control impulses, thinking before acting.
- Recognize negative feelings and express them in an appropriate manner.

Self-talk and self-instruction seems to be effective in many situations. Here is an example of self-talk:

I am feeling angry. I want to hit him. If I hit him, he will hit me and Mr. Marks will scold me. I will walk away until I feel better.

The related component is to be responsible for one's own behavior. Statements such as the following indicate that a person is feeling responsible:

- I teased you. It made you feel bad. I am sorry I teased you.
- I pushed Willy. He fell down. I am sorry I pushed him.
- I did not do my homework. I held up the rest of our group. I am sorry I did not do my homework.

The statements include three steps, which all start with "A:"

- *Admit* the misbehavior
- *Acknowledge* the consequences
- *Apologize* for the misbehavior

This simple formula can be taught to all students so that they can contribute to a classroom environment that teaches responsibility.

APPRECIATING SIMILARITIES AND DIFFERENCES

Anthropologists believe in a set of statements that need to be posted in all classrooms.

- All people are alike

  Every individual shares important characteristics with all other humans. This first lesson—that all humans are alike in several ways—is particularly significant for students with disabilities, who tend to be too aware of their differentness.

♦ Some people are alike

Members of the same ethnic group tend to share a common culture. However, overemphasizing group similarities can be risky, because it can easily lead students to believe in unwarranted stereotypes. Thus, not all Asian students are highly intelligent, even though they are so stereotyped.

♦ No two people are the same

Everyone is a unique individual. Even "identical" twins are not completely alike.

Teachers interested in developing an awareness of human similarities, group commonalities, and individual differences have several options available to them: modeling; teaching; making rules; and using the hidden curriculum.

♦ Modeling

The teacher can be a strong role model. Avoiding favoritism teaches the importance of similarities. Recognizing individual students operationalizes an awareness of students' uniqueness.

♦ Teaching

Developing concepts and using activities that emphasize the value of both similarities and differences can influence student attitudes. For example, teachers report that using "Strength Graphs" help students appreciate differences. A portion of a Strength Graph is shown in Figure 4.2.

FIGURE 4.2. PORTION OF A STRENGTH GRAPH

Very strong

Strong

Average

Not strong

Needs
Development

Physical   Math   Nature   Reading Planning

The teacher helps the students identify areas where
people can be strong or weak. Here is a sample list:

- Being physically strong
- Doing mathematics
- Understanding nature
- Reading, writing, and speaking
- Planning and managing a project
- Getting along with and helping others
- Playing music and singing
- Making things in wood, fabric, metal, and other
  materials

In helping students develop such a list, keep in
mind that you want a list that will help the students
see that all of them have strengths and weaknesses.

The teacher can then model the desired behavior by
completing his or her own Strength Graph, showing

relative strengths and weaknesses. The Strength Graph teaches two critical lessons: We need each other and everyone has strengths and weaknesses.

♦ Making rules

At times very explicit rules need to be made and re-inforced. One researcher found, for example, that this rule helped younger students understand in-clusiveness: "You don't say 'You can't play.'" (Paley, 1992). As noted below, teachers should involve stu-dents in making rules for their class.

♦ Using the hidden curriculum

As explained in Chapter 3, the hidden curriculum is the lessons imparted by the culture and procedures of the school, which have a strong impact on the learners. For example, student art work hanging in the corridor sends this message: We value student creativity. Ensuring that the art work has been cre-ated by students of varied ethnicity and special strengths shows that the school values diversity. As Ryan (1992) put it, "While unseen, the hidden cur-riculum must be considered with the same serious-ness as the written, formal curriculum" (p. 18).

COOPERATING AND COLLABORATING

All students need to learn how to work and learn together, especially in cooperative groups. Several types of cooperative learning result in better learning, improved interpersonal atti-tudes, and more appropriate social behaviors. (See Johnson & Johnson, 1991; Slavin, 1990; and Zemelman, Daniels, & Hyde, 1998).

Although as many as nine different types of cooperative learning have been identified, most have certain features in common. Those features can provide useful guidelines for teachers using cooperative groups with students with disabili-ties.

♦ Identify the group task

Groups can achieve several tasks: read together, give each other feedback on student products, teach each other, share experiences, discuss ideas, solve problems, respond to teacher's questions. Be sure that the group has a clear understanding of the task. (For more on performance tasks, see Chapter 8.)

♦ Use a group structure appropriate for the task

Four choices are available here: whole class, including students with disabilities; small heterogeneous groups, with one or two students with disabilities in each group; cluster groups of four or five students with disabilities working together. In general, heterogeneous groups will produce greater benefits for students with disabilities. (See Oakes, Wells, Yonezawa, & Ray, 1997.)

Suppose, for example, the teacher expects the students to solve a complex problem in the community. Using the whole class is inappropriate, because there are too many students in the class; large groups have difficulty solving problems. Individuals working on their own will face many obstacles, because the problem is too complex for one individual. A heterogeneous small group would seem to be the best choice.

♦ Use an accountability program that holds both the group and individual students responsible

Group performance can be assessed by evaluating their products. Individuals can be held accountable through peer evaluation, individual examinations, and reports on work accomplished.

♦ Monitor the groups as they work

Give the group appropriate feedback about both process and content. Be especially concerned with the learning and behavior of any students with disabilities.

All students, but particularly students with disabilities, will need to be trained in the skills of effective group work. The following skills are best taught in context, as those skills are needed in carrying out group work:

- Staying focused on the task
- Being clear about the goal
- Actively contributing to the group
- Taking turns when speaking
- Listening actively
- Monitoring group progress
- Evaluating group and individual effectiveness

EXPERIENCING A CURRICULUM OF COMMUNITY

The learning community can also be enhanced by a curriculum that helps students develop knowledge about communities and share the values upon which communities are grounded.

As explained more fully in Chapter 6, this work recommends a three-part curriculum for students with disabilities: the regular curriculum, as adapted; the special curriculum, designed only for students with disabilities; and the individual curriculum, developed for an individual student. The *curriculum of community* could be developed as part of the regular curriculum, adapted for students with disabilities, or as part of the special curriculum as a series of units taught at each level. Here are some of the titles of interdisciplinary units that teachers might design, with a suggested allocation:

Grade 1.   Our Family as a Community

Grade 2.   Our Neighborhood as a Community

Grade 3.   Creating a Community of Friends

Grade 4.   Working out Differences in our Community

Grade 5.   Learning to Work Together in a Classroom Community

Grade 6.   Learning to Trust and Respect

Grade 7.   Making our School a Better Community

Grade 8.   Solving Problems in the Classroom Community

Grade 9. Communities around the World

Grade 10. Everyone Is Special in a Good Community

Grade 11. Utopian Communities in the Past

Grade 12. The Workplace as a Community

Other topics and grade allocations are possible, of course. The critical consideration is to be sure that all students with disabilities have an opportunity to know about the concept of community and to operationalize it to the extent of their abilities.

LEARNING IN AN INVITING ENVIRONMENT

The optimal climate for students with disabilities is a warm and inviting one. The concept of an *inviting environment* has several related dimensions. First, it is an environment that invites students with disabilities to come in and learn with inviting materials. Varied media are readily available and easy to use. Assistive technology is there to accommodate the needs of the students who need it. A varied collection of books and other materials helps all students understand and accept those with special needs. Materials have been chosen that represent and value the ethnic diversity of that classroom. And the learning materials are of high quality, of interest to students, and of a range of difficulty.

Second, the physical environment is inviting. The classroom looks inviting. The work of students with disabilities is often posted on bulletin boards. Messages around the room are positive and inviting: "You are welcome to use these books with care." Bright colors have been used to make the classroom look warm and inviting. Ample space sends a clear message: "There is room for you here."

Finally, it is an inviting "people environment." All are meant to feel welcome. (See Child Development Project, 1994.) Parents especially are invited to come. And volunteers from the neighborhood are recruited to bring a fresh perspective to the instructional team.

USING THE POWER OF
DISABLED STUDENTS TO
AFFECT THEIR OWN EDUCATION

A learning community is a democratic community. A democratic school has the following conditions and attributes (as paraphrased from Beane & Apple, 1995):

- The open flow of ideas, to enable people to be fully informed.
- Faith in the individual and collective capacity of people to resolve problems.
- The use of critical reflection to evaluate proposals, policies, and solutions.
- Concern for the common good.
- Concern for the dignity and rights of all people.
- An understanding that democracy is a set of values to be lived.
- The organization of social institutions to promote the democratic way of life.

As those authors point out, several schools have operationalized those conditions in creating and maintaining democratic schools.

Can students with disabilities participate in democratic processes? Educators who share democratic values have found that students with disabilities can and should participate to the extent of their abilities. Teachers report that students with disabilities in an inclusive classroom, for example, can understand and participate in rule-making for the class.

A CONCLUDING NOTE

Good learning can take place in a variety of environments and under varied conditions. However, teachers who can create a classroom learning community have a special edge.

REFERENCES

Beane, J. A., & Apple, M. W. (1995). The case for democratic schools. In M. W. Apple & J. A. Beane (Eds.), *Democratic schools* (pp. 1–25). Alexandria, VA: Association for Supervision and Curriculum Development.

Child Development Project. (1994). *At home in our schools: A guide to schoolwide activities that build community.* Oakland, CA: Developmental Studies Center.

Good, T. L., & Brophy, J. E. (1997). *Looking in classrooms* (7th ed.). New York: Longman.

Johnson, D. W., & Johnson, R. T. (1991). *Learning together and alone.* Englewood Cliffs, NJ: Prentice Hall.

McGregor, G., & Vogelsberg, R. T. (1998). *Inclusive schooling practices: Pedagogical and research foundations.* Baltimore: Brookes.

Oakes, J., Wells, A. S., Yonezawa, S., & Ray, K. (1997). Equity lessons from detracking schools. In A. Hargreaves (Ed.), *Rethinking educational change with heart and mind.* Alexandria, VA: Association for Supervision and Curriculum Development.

Paley, V. (1992). *You can't say you can't play.* Cambridge, MA: Harvard University Press.

Ryan, K. (1992). Mining the values in the classroom. *Educational Leadership, 54* (1), 16–18.

Sergiovanni, T. (1994). *Building community in schools.* San Francisco: Jossey-Bass.

Slavin, R. E. (1990). *Cooperative learning: Theory, research, and practice.* Englewood Cliffs, NJ: Prentice Hall.

Zemelman, S., Daniels, H., & Hyde, A. (1998). *Best practice* (2d ed.). Portsmouth, NH: Heinemann.

5

ASSESSING OPPORTUNITY STANDARDS AND ACCEPTING THE CONSTRAINTS

In developing and delivering special education programs, leaders need both to provide opportunities and accept the constraints. The opportunities are generally provided by the local school system; the constraints are chiefly imposed through federal regulations. This chapter explains both the opportunities and the constraints.

OPPORTUNITY STANDARDS FOR SPECIAL EDUCATION

As explained in Chapter 1, an opportunity standard is a statement of the opportunities and supports that are required if the student is to achieve the performance standard. Consider this example of two blind students. John has an opportunity to use voice recognition software and a computer; Susan still uses a typewriter. Obviously that opportunity difference will result in a difference in their ability to write.

Should all students have an equal opportunity? They should, of course, if "equal opportunity" is construed as the equal opportunity for all students to achieve their full potential. However, that principle will clearly result in several seeming inequities. Meeting the special needs of students with disabilities will require additional resources—small classes, special equipment, additional time, and special personnel.

MEETING THE OPPORTUNITY STANDARDS

The following opportunity standards for students with disabilities have been synthesized from a review of the literature (as noted below) and the experience of these authors, as filtered through our own value system.

All students with disabilities *need the opportunity...*

♦ To learn in the most supportive school environment.

For almost all students with disabilities that environment will be an inclusive classroom in a school committed to the values of inclusiveness (McGregor & Vogelsberg, 1998).

♦ To learn from effective teachers who care about them and accept them as individuals.

Acceptance is especially important. The best teachers accept students with disabilities as individuals, not members of a "handicapped" group (Janney & Snell, 1996).

♦ To learn from a standards-based curriculum that emphasizes problem solving and is adapted to their special needs.

In too many instances, schools have offered students with disabilities a second-class curriculum (McDonnell, McLaughlin, & Morison, 1997).

♦ To have sufficient time to achieve at the performance standard specified.

The block schedule and other scheduling alternatives that provide larger blocks of time seem to be especially helpful to students with disabilities (Canady & Rettig, 1995).

♦ To be provided with the needed learning resources.

In addition to trained personnel and ample time, students with disabilities should be provided with the books they need, the computers they require, and the software and media that will assist them in the learning process (McDonnell & McLaughlin, 1997).

♦ To have valid assessment that recognizes their disability, that provides developmental feedback when needed, and enables them to demonstrate their learning (Fuchs, 1994).

These general opportunity standards, of course, need to be more clearly specified at the local and individual levels.

ACCEPTING THE CONSTRAINTS: THE INDIVIDUALIZED EDUCATIONAL PROGRAM

Special educators do not have total freedom to do whatever they think is best. Instead, they are governed by very specific and constraining federal regulations, the most important of which are examined below.

The first constraint is the form and content of the Individualized Educational Program (IEP). In enacting the IDEA Amendment of 1997, Congress found that research and best practice over the past twenty years have demonstrated that an effective educational system must maintain high academic standards and clear performance goals for children with disabilities, consistent with the standards and expectations for all students. Congress also concluded that schools should provide for appropriate and effective strategies to ensure that disabled students have maximum opportunities to achieve these standards and goals. Accordingly, federal legislation continues to emphasize the importance of the Individualized Educational Program.

THE IEP TEAM

Federal regulations specify the composition of the IEP team, those responsible for developing and implementing the IEP. The IEP team should include the following members:

- The parent of the child with the disability.
- At least one regular education teacher of such child (if the child is, or may be, participating in the regular education environment).
- At least one special education teacher, or where appropriate, at least one special education provider of services.
- A representative of the local education agency who is qualified to provide, or supervise the provision of, specially designed instruction who is also knowledgeable about the general curriculum and the availability of resources of the local educational agency.

- ♦ An individual who can interpret the instructional implications of evaluation.
- ♦ At the discretion of the parent or the agency, other individuals who have knowledge or special expertise regarding the child, including related service personnel as appropriate.
- ♦ Whenever appropriate, the child with the disability (IDEA, 1997).

COMPONENTS OF THE IEP

Regulations also specify the components of the IEP, as follows:

- ♦ The child's present level of performance.
- ♦ The child's disability and how the disability affects involvement and progress in the general curriculum. For preschool children the IEP must state how the disability affects the child's participation in appropriate activities.
- ♦ Measurable goals related to the child's needs. In achieving those goals the child should be involved and make progress in the general curriculum.
- ♦ The short-term objectives (measurable, intermediate steps) and major milestones or benchmarks in order to measure progress during the school year (IDEA, 1997).

Chapter 11 explains how to relate the IEP to a standards-based curriculum.

LEAST-RESTRICTIVE ENVIRONMENT

To the extent appropriate, children with disabilities (including children in public or private institutions or other care facilities) should be educated with children who are not disabled. Special classes, separate schooling, or other removal of children with disabilities from the regular educational environment are provided only when the nature or severity of the disability is such that education in regular classes with the use of supplementary aides and services cannot be achieved satisfactorily.

Supplementary aids and services include supports provided in regular classrooms that enable the child with disabilities to be educated with nondisabled children (IDEA, 1997).

TRANSITION SERVICES

When the child reaches the age of 14, the IEP must include a statement of the transition services needed. Transition services are a coordinated set of activities that promote movement from school to postschool activities. These services include instruction, related services, community experiences, the development of employment skills and other adult living objectives, and when appropriate, acquisition of daily living skills. At least one year before a disabled youth reaches the age of majority, he or she must be informed about his or her rights under this law. The disabled person must also be informed about any rights that will transfer to the student on reaching the age of majority (IDEA, 1997).

Beginning at age 16 (or younger) as determined by the IEP team, a statement of needed transition services for the child shall include, when appropriate, a statement of the interagency responsibilities or any needed linkages.

REPORTING OF PROGRESS ON THE IEP

The IEP must include a statement of how the child's progress toward the annual goals will be measured and how the parents will be regularly informed. They must be informed at least as often as parents of nondisabled students. Parent information could take the form of a six- or nine-week report card. They must be notified of the extent to which the child's progress is sufficient to enable him or her to achieve the goals by the end of the school year (IDEA, 1997).

ASSESSMENT

The IEP must include a statement of any individual modifications in the administration of state or district-wide assessment of student achievement that are needed in order for the child to participate. If the IEP team decides that the child will not participate in a particular assessment, then a statement must be included as to why that assessment is not appropriate and which alternative assessments will be administered. The 1997 Amendment also states that the public must be informed as to the number participating in general and alternative assessments and how the students performed on such assessments.

ROLE OF THE PARENT

One of the key purposes of the IDEA Amendments of 1997 was to expand and promote opportunities for parents and professionals to work in new partnerships. The parents of the child with a disability are expected to be equal participants along with school personnel in developing, reviewing, and revising the IEP for their child. Parents should take an active role in providing critical information about their child's abilities, interests, performance, and history. They should be equal participants in the discussion about their child's need for special education, related services, and supplementary aids and devices. They aid in deciding how their child will be involved in the general curriculum and in state and districtwide assessments. They will cooperate in identifying what services their child will be provided and in what setting. They will be invited to participate in meetings about their child's identification, evaluation, development of the IEP, and educational placement. They participate in deciding what additional data are needed as part of the evaluation of their child and bring any concerns or information that will be helpful in developing and reviewing their child's IEP. Parents must be informed who the participants will be at the IEP meeting, as well as the purpose, time, and location of the meeting. Parents have the right to receive a copy of their child's IEP (IDEA, 1997).

EXTENDED SCHOOL YEAR

The IEP team must decide on an annual basis whether a particular student requires extended school year programming and if so, what those special education services will be. The need for extended school year is made on a case-by-case basis. A school system may not refuse to offer these services based solely on the fact that it doesn't want to, doesn't have the staff, or can't afford it.

Special Considerations in Developing an IEP

Federal regulations also specify other considerations in developing an IEP. The IEP team is required to develop appropriate strategies, including positive behavioral intervention for a child whose behavior impedes his or her learning or that of others. In the case of a child with limited English proficiency, the language needs of the child as it relates to the IEP must be considered. When a child is blind or visually impaired, instruction in Braille must be provided unless the IEP team determines, after an evaluation of the child's reading and writing skills, that instruction in Braille is not appropriate. If a child is deaf or hard of hearing, the language and communication needs of the child must be considered, including opportunities for direct communication with peers and professional personnel in the child's language. The school also must provide opportunities for direct instruction in the child's language. A final special consideration governs the need for special technology devices or services. If the IEP team determines that a child needs a particular device or service, then the team must include a statement to that effect in the child's IEP (IDEA, 1997).

Other Regulations

In addition to specifying the components of the IEP, federal regulations control other aspects of the special learner's education.

Protections for Children Not Yet Eligible for Services

A child not yet eligible for special education services who violates the school's conduct code may have protections under the law. Several claims must be supported with suitable evidence, as follows: the parents had expressed a concern in writing that the child was suspected of having a disability or parents had requested an evaluation, or the child's behavior indicated a need, or the teacher or other personnel had expressed a concern (IDEA, 1997).

INITIAL EVALUATIONS

Parents must be provided notice of a intent to evaluate, and their signature on a statement of informed consent must be obtained. No single procedure shall be the sole criterion for determining eligibility in a special program. The child must be assessed in all areas of the suspected disability, and determination of eligibility shall be made by a team of qualified professionals, along with the child's parent. The child may not be determined eligible if the sole deciding factor is a lack of math or reading instruction or if the child has limited English proficiency (IDEA, 1997).

REEVALUATION

A reevaluation must be conducted at least every three years. Informed consent must be obtained, but reevaluation may proceed if the school district demonstrates a reasonable effort to obtain the consent. Existing data must be reviewed to determine if any additional data are needed to determine continued eligibility and necessity for modifications in the program. If no additional data are needed, then parents will be notified of the determination and of their right to request an assessment. The school district is not required to conduct an assessment unless requested by the parent (IDEA, 1997).

DISCIPLINE

School personnel may order a change in placement to an alternative setting for not more than 45 days if the student brings a weapon to school or if the student possesses, uses, or sells controlled substances or illegal drugs. If the school district has not conducted a functional behavioral assessment and implemented a behavioral intervention plan, then one must be completed no later than 10 days after the disciplinary action is taken. A functional assessment allows school personnel to understand what causes a problem behavior and how to prevent it from occurring or designing procedures for responding to the behavior when it does occur. While in an alternative educational setting, the child must be provided all services stated in the child's IEP (IDEA, 1997).

A manifestation determination must be conducted for any other disciplinary actions that result in a change of placement for more than 10 days for other violations of the school conduct code. If school personnel decide that the disability did not impair the child's ability to understand the impact and consequences of behavior and the disability did not impair the child's ability to control behavior, then general discipline measures apply (IDEA, 1997).

A CONCLUDING NOTE

Many educators feel frustrated at the seemingly tight federal control of special education. Though such frustration is understandable, two considerations should be noted. First, those regulations have resulted in significant improvements in the education of special children and youth. Second, federal fiscal support for special education warrants federal control. In essence, those who provide the money have a right to say how the money will be spent.

REFERENCES

Canady, R. L., & Rettig, M. D. (1995). *Block scheduling: A catalyst for change in high schools.* Larchmont, NY: Eye on Education.

Fuchs, L. S. (1994). *Connecting performance assessment to instruction.* Reston, VA: Council for Exceptional Children.

Individuals With Disabilities Education Act, 34 C.F.R. part 300 (1997).

Janney, R. E., & Snell, M. E. (1996). How teachers use peer interactions to include students with mild and severe disabilities in elementary general education classes. *Journal of the Association for Persons with Severe Disabilities, 21* (2), 72–80.

McGregor, G., & Vogelsberg, R. T. (1998). *Inclusive schooling practices: Pedagogical and research foundations.* Baltimore: Brookes.

McDonnell, L. M., McLaughlin, M. J., & Morison, P. (Eds.) (1997). *Educating one and all.* Washington, DC: National Academy Press.

PART III

THE KEY FACTORS

6

USING CURRICULUM STANDARDS

There is much talk these days about a standards-based curriculum. *Curriculum standards* are statements of the content that students are to learn in one subject for all grades or levels. Special educators and school administrators are currently debating the issue of whether a single standards-based curriculum should be provided for all students or whether students with disabilities need a curriculum designed for them alone. Those arguing for a single curriculum believe that an inclusive curriculum that uses the same standards for all students is the best way to operationalize the core concepts of inclusion. Those arguing for special standards for students with disabilities believe that the uniqueness of students with disabilities warrants the development of a special education curriculum based upon special standards. The position taken here is that students with disabilities deserve a differentiated standards-based curriculum, one that builds upon the common curriculum but adapts and supplements it in special ways. As explained further below, such a curriculum is like a pie that has one part regular, one part special, and one part individual.

This chapter provides the knowledge and skills that you need to develop a standards-based curriculum for students with disabilities.

ACQUIRING THE ESSENTIAL KNOWLEDGE

You need to know three types of foundation knowledge—about the types of curriculum; about standards; and about performance tasks and assessments.

TYPES OF CURRICULUM

Curriculum is one of those common terms that educators use freely without understanding all that is implied by the concept. As Figure 6.1 shows, there really are eight kinds of curricula that can be identified.

FIGURE 6.1. TYPES OF CURRICULA

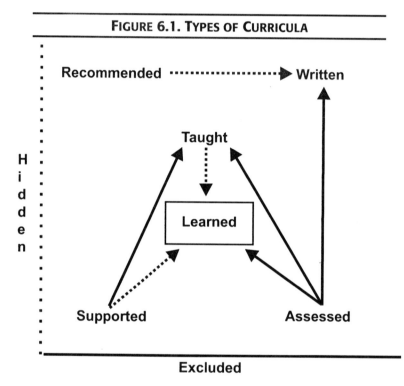

Code: Dotted line represents weak influence; solid line represents strong influence

---

♦ Recommended Curriculum

This is the curriculum content that experts recommend; in most cases the experts are scholars in the subject field who have a special interest in schooling. Their recommendations are usually promulgated through the various professional organizations to which they belong, such as the National Council for the Social Studies and the National Council of Teachers of Mathematics. Kendall and Marzano's book, *Content Knowledge* (1997), is an excellent compilation of such recommended standards.

♦ Written Curriculum

This term is used to identify the documents produced by the state, the local school district, the school, and the teacher to guide the teacher about what to teach. A district curriculum guide is the most commonly used example of the written curriculum.

♦ Taught Curriculum

This is the curriculum that the teacher actually presents day by day. In deciding what to teach, most teachers give careful consideration to their students' needs, their knowledge of what has worked before, the tests that will be given, and the materials they have available. They tend to see the district curriculum guide only as a reminder of what they should emphasize.

♦ Learned Curriculum

This might be termed the "bottom line" curriculum, because in the final analysis it is the only curriculum that matters—what students actually learn. Even with effective teachers, there is often a gap between the taught and the learned curricula, because students are not always attentive and do not always understand what is being taught.

♦ Supported Curriculum

This is the curriculum that appears in textbooks, software, and multimedia. Because elementary teachers in self-contained classrooms usually have to teach all four academic subjects, they tend to rely on the text, especially in areas where they are not strong in content knowledge.

♦ Assessed Curriculum

This is the curriculum that appears in tests and other forms of assessment. Teachers are especially concerned about preparing their students for "high stakes" tests given by the state, because such tests are often used to evaluate school and individual teacher effectiveness.

♦ Hidden Curriculum

As explained in Chapter 3, such a curriculum is hidden because most administrators and teachers are unaware of it.

♦ Excluded Curriculum

This is the curriculum content that has been left out—either intentionally or unintentionally. One of the best places to examine the excluded curriculum is the curriculum in U.S. history. Most history texts and curriculum guides exclude such topics as the place of religion in American life and the role of the labor movement. Many students with disabilities have never experienced a Shakespeare play; it has been excluded from their curriculum because some teachers unwisely consider it "over their heads."

What are the implications of this analysis for the curriculum of students with disabilities? Curriculum builders should:

♦ Focus on the learned curriculum; ensure that students with disabilities master an appropriate and a quality curriculum.

♦ Give special attention to the taught curriculum, as it is the major element influencing the learned. Use instructional methods that build on the strengths of students with disabilities.

♦ Provide a multifaceted written curriculum to meet the needs of students with disabilities.

♦ Structure the supported curriculum so that students with disabilities use materials and resources that facilitate their learning.

- Ensure that the assessed curriculum for students with disabilities measures only what they have had an opportunity to learn.

- Ensure that the hidden curriculum sends positive messages to students with disabilities. Check especially on the terms that classroom teachers and regular students use to talk about students with disabilities.

- Include in the special curriculum, topics that have been unwisely excluded. Set high expectations for what students with disabilities can learn.

STANDARDS

Some dictionaries list as many as 10 definitions of this complex term. This is the one used here: *A statement of what is educationally desirable.* Three types of standards are used in discussing educational matters.

- Curriculum Standards

  These statements indicate what students are expected to learn. Sometimes they are called *content standards.* In current usage, most curriculum standards specify what students are to learn by the end of grade 12 in one subject, rather than what teachers are to teach. Here is an example from science:

  - Knows the basic features of the earth.

  Curriculum standards are further analyzed into *benchmarks.* In discussing curriculum, a benchmark is one component of a curriculum standard, usually identified for a group of grade levels or a specific grade. Here is an example of a Grades 3 to 5 benchmark that results from analyzing the science standard about the earth:

  - Knows the major differences between fresh and ocean waters.

- Performance Standards

  A performance standard is a statement of the level of student performance that will be considered acceptable. An example of a performance standard is the minimum score on the Graduate Record Examination that a university will accept for admission to graduate studies. Here is an example of a performance standard for a student with a disability studying ocean and fresh water:

- Correctly specifies one difference between fresh and ocean waters.

♦ Opportunity Standards

As explained in Chapter 5, an opportunity standard is a statement of the supports required for the student to achieve the performance standard with respect to a given curriculum standard. Here is an example of an opportunity standard for students with disabilities:

- The students with disabilities will experience a curriculum that has been adapted to respond to their special needs.

The point is to ensure that the learners have the opportunity to achieve the performance standard.

PERFORMANCE TASKS AND ASSESSMENTS

After the curriculum standards and their benchmarks have been identified, you need to define the performance task and its performance assessment.

PERFORMANCE TASKS

A *performance task* is an open-ended problem that students solve, using the knowledge they have acquired. Here are some examples of performance tasks that some students with disabilities could accomplish.

♦ Draw a map showing how to get from your house to your school or your school bus stop.

♦ Suppose that your dog needs a fenced in place. You decide to make the space 20 feet long and 10 feet wide. How much fencing would you need?

♦ Suppose that you were a Native American back in the time of Columbus. What do you think you would have felt about the arrival of the white people? Make a recording of what your thoughts would have been.

PERFORMANCE ASSESSMENTS

A performance assessment is an evaluation of how successfully the student has completed the performance task. Here are some ways you can make a performance assessment of students with disabilities.

♦ Interview the student.

♦ Have the student answer written questions.

♦ Evaluate a product the student has produced, such as a letter, or a model, or a speech.

♦ Observe the student as he or she demonstrates what has been learned.

In assessing the performance you should develop and apply *rubrics*. A rubric is a scoring guide to help you and the student know what qualities will be assessed. Figure 6.2 (p. 88) shows part of the rubrics for the task of making a map cited above.

UNDERSTANDING THE HALLMARKS OF A QUALITY SPECIAL EDUCATION CURRICULUM

A review of the literature and an analysis of our experience suggest that the following features would be found in a quality curriculum for students with disabilities. (See, for example, Ford, Davern, & Schnorr, 1992; Mastropieri & Scroggs, 1992; and Schrag, 1993.)

♦ A significant part of the curriculum is based on the same standards used in developing the regular curriculum. Those standards will be addressed by making such adaptations as using alternative instructional methods and providing additional time.

FIGURE 6.2. RUBRICS: DRAWING MAP

Criteria	Performance Rating	Indicators
1. Comprehensiveness	Excellent: A	Includes all components: orientation; location of school or bus stop; location of home; route numbers; road names; distances
	Very good: B	Includes five components
	More than satisfactory: C	Includes four components
	Satisfactory: D	Includes three components
	Poor: F	Includes 1 or 2 components

♦ A major part of the curriculum has been developed for students with disabilities in general, to the extent that their needs can be predicted.

♦ The unique needs of individual students are addressed through an individual curriculum.

♦ The curriculum gives sufficient attention to the life skills that students with disabilities need to function effectively in society.

♦ The curriculum gives students with disabilities access to a meaningful present and a hopeful future. It is not a dead-end curriculum, but is instead one that opens doors.

♦ The curriculum is flexible and provides a sound basis for Individualized Educational Programs.

♦ The basic special education curriculum is coordinated from grade to grade, so that the curriculum for the present grade builds upon that for the previous grade and leads to the one for the next grade. Note that throughout this book the term *grade* is used to designate a level of curriculum, in order to achieve clarity. However; all placements for purposes of instruction should be individualized, without concern for the student's grade level. Also, the use of the term *grade* makes it easier to communicate with regular classroom teachers and should facilitate inclusion.

♦ The curriculum gives students with disabilities structured experiences in solving problems that are real for them.

♦ The curriculum is structured so that students with disabilities can achieve mastery and learn in relative depth, rather than leading to superficial coverage.

THE THREE-PART CURRICULUM: THE REGULAR CURRICULUM

These quality indicators can perhaps best be achieved through a curriculum supported by three parts: the *regular* curriculum, the *special* curriculum, and the *individual* curriculum. The contrasts between the three types are summarized in Figure 6.3 (p. 90) and shown diagrammatically in Figure 6.4 (p. 90).

FIGURE 6.3. SUMMARY OF THREE-PART CURRICULUM

Aspect	*Regular*	*Special*	*Individual*
Source of standards and benchmarks	Selected from the district curriculum	Added from professional literature	Added from analysis of individual need
Identified by	Curriculum task force, with input from teaching teams	Curriculum task force, with input from teaching teams	IEP committee

FIGURE 6.4. THREE CURRICULUM PARTS

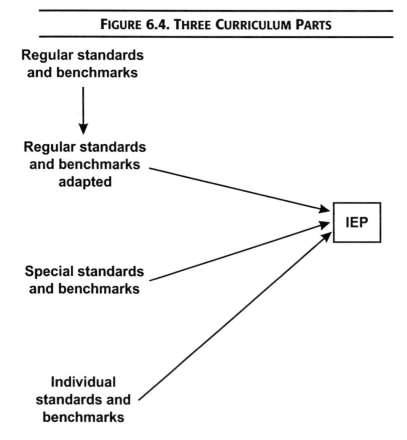

Regular standards and benchmarks

Regular standards and benchmarks adapted

Special standards and benchmarks

Individual standards and benchmarks

IEP

As the name implies, the regular curriculum is the common curriculum provided to all students. (For a full explanation of how to develop a regular standards-based curriculum, see Glatthorn, 1999.) As an inclusive curriculum, it is built from selected standards and benchmarks offered to all students. However, its standards and benchmarks are offered to students with disabilities with certain noncurricular adaptations. To understand the types of adaptations, consider this standard and its benchmark for the subject Civics, Grades 6 to 8 (Kendall & Marzano, 1997).

- ◆ Standard

    Understands the role of diversity in American life and the importance of shared values, political beliefs, and civic beliefs in an increasingly diverse American society.

- ◆ Grade 7 Benchmark

    Knows a variety of forms of diversity in American society.

You can adapt this common benchmark for students with disabilities by modifying eight components. You can identify a simpler performance task. You can lower the performance standard. You can provide an alternative performance assessment. You can provide additional time for students with disabilities. You can use alternative learning materials. You can change the teaching/learning method. You can change the instructor, using the special educator or a peer, rather than the classroom teacher. Finally, you can use an alternative group structure, using whole class for general students and small group for students with disabilities. Cooperative learning is especially effective with students with disabilities. The types of adaptation you choose will, of course, depend on the needs and strengths of students with disabilities and the nature of the skills and concepts to be learned. Figure 6.5 (p. 92) summarizes the types of adaptations.

FIGURE 6.5. ADAPTATION ANALYSIS:
REGULAR CURRICULUM FOR STUDENTS WITH DISABILITIES

- ◆ *Standard:* Understand role of diversity and importance of shared values.
- ◆ *Benchmark:* Knows a variety of forms of diversity in American life.

Type of Adaptation	For Regular Learners	For Students with Disabilities
Performance Task	Write essay explaining how you are the same but different.	Discuss with other students how you are the same but different.
Performance Standard	Identify 6 similarities and 6 differences.	Identify 4 similarities and 4 differences.
Performance Assessment	Develop, provide rubrics; grade essays accordingly.	Explain simplified rubrics; observe discussion.
Time for Learning	One instructional period.	Two instructional periods.
Learning Materials	Social studies textbook.	Videocassette, "Same but different."
Learning Method	Read text; write essay, "How I am the same but different."	View video cassette; discuss, "How I am the same but different."
Instructor	Regular teacher.	Special educator.
Group Structure	Whole class or small group.	Cooperative groups or individualized learning.

The regular curriculum for students with disabilities can be developed by a Special Education Curriculum Task Force, using the following process. First, the task force would begin by reviewing all the state and school district standards for all students. They would use these criteria to select the regular standards to be used for students with disabilities:

- Importance and usefulness for the students with disabilities
- Developmental appropriateness, within the developmental ability of students with disabilities to achieve, given suitable adaptations
- Importance to that subject
- Likelihood of appearing on state tests

For example, here are the Life Sciences standards from the Kendall-Marzano (1997) compilation:

1. Knows about the diversity and unity that characterize life.
2. Understands the genetic basis for the transfer of biological characteristics from one generation to the next.
3. Knows the general structure and functions of cells in organisms.
4. Understands how species depend on one another and the environment for survival.
5. Understands the cycling of matter and flow of energy through the living environment.
6. Understands the basic concepts of the evolution of species.

Here the task force might identify Standards 1, 4, and 5 as appropriate for students with disabilities.

The next step is to select the benchmarks to be mastered at each grade, using the same criteria. Suppose, for example, that the district science curriculum lists these four benchmarks for Standard 4, Grade 5:

4.1.   Knows that the behavior of individual organisms is influenced by internal and external cues and that humans and other organisms have senses to detect these cues.

4.2.   Knows that an organism's behavior is related to the environment.

4.3.   Knows that changes in the environment have different effects on different organisms.

4.4.   Knows that all organisms cause changes in the environment.

The task force might decide to use Benchmarks 4.3 and 4.4.

THE THREE-PART CURRICULUM: THE SPECIAL CURRICULUM

The special curriculum should be seen as a quality program, specifically designed for students with disabilities. The following process can be used here.

IDENTIFYING STANDARDS

The task force would begin by identifying the special standards for students with disabilities. Those standards would include modifications of the district standards and additional standards not included in the regular curriculum. The modifications would be made chiefly by simplifying the district standards. The new standards would be made by utilizing three different sources: the state standards for special education; the needs of students with disabilities as identified by the task force and the IEP committee; teaching teams; and the professional literature on special education. (Loyd & Brolin (1997) is an excellent source for recommended adaptations.)

Whereas the regular curriculum for students with disabilities selects from the district standards, the special curriculum is developed by modifying or adding to the standards. As an example, consider the Kendall-Marzano standards for K–4, US history, as shown in Figure 6.6. (Although most standards speak to a K–12 curriculum, Kendall and Marzano choose to identify different standards for particular grade levels.) Figure 6.6 shows the standards used in the regular curriculum and, in parentheses, the changes and additions made by the task force.

FIGURE 6.6. STANDARDS K–4: US HISTORY

---

1. Understands family life now and in the past, and family life in various places years ago.

   (SPECIAL CURRICULUM: Understands American family life now and in grandparents' era.)

2. Understands the history of the local community and how communities in North America varied long ago.

   (SPECIAL CURRICULUM: Understands history of local community.)

3. Understands the people, events, problems, and ideas that were significant in creating the history of their state.

   (SPECIAL CURRICULUM: Understands people and events that were significant in creating the history of their state.)

4. Understands how democratic values came to be, and how they have been exemplified by people, events, and symbols.

   (SPECIAL CURRICULUM: Understands democratic values.)

5. Understands the causes and nature of movements of large groups of people into and within the United States, now and long ago.

   (SPECIAL CURRICULUM: Understands why people come to live in the United States.)

6. Understands the folklore and other cultural contributions from various regions of the United States and how they helped form a national heritage.

   (SPECIAL CURRICULUM: Understands the folklore of selected regions of the United States.)

(Figure continues on next page.)

7. Understands selected attributes and historical developments of societies in Africa, the Americas, Asia, and Europe.

   (SPECIAL CURRICULUM: Understands present conditions in other regions of the world: one in Africa, one in the Americas, one in Asia, and one in Europe.)

8. Understands major discoveries in science and technology, some of their social and economic effects and the major scientists and inventors responsible for them.

   (MODIFY: Understands major discoveries in science and technology and their impact on society.)

9. STANDARD TO BE ADDED: Understands that many great people have had special limitations.

(Original standards paraphrased from Kendall & Marzano, 1997, p. 116.)

IDENTIFYING THE BENCHMARKS

The next critical task is to identify the grade level benchmarks for students with disabilities. The simplest way to identify benchmarks for each grade is for the task force to make the initial decisions by analyzing the standards and considering the developmental abilities of students with disabilities. Consider, for example, this standard from the special curriculum:

Understands family life now and in grandparents' era.

Here are the elementary benchmarks that could be identified by analysis:

♦ Grade 3: Understand how families work together now.

Understands how families worked together in grandparents' era.

♦ Grade 4: Understands how families entertain themselves now.

Understands how families entertained themselves in grandparents' era.

♦ Grade 5: Understands how families get information now.

Understands how families got information in grandparents' era.

The task force would then ask all educators involved with special education to review their decisions. Interested parents should also be invited to review the tentative list of benchmarks. A form similar to the one shown in Figure 6.7 can be used to survey educators and parents.

FIGURE 6.7. SAMPLE SURVEY FORM:
TEACHERS AND PARENTS

As you may know, we are developing a new curriculum for our students with disabilities. We would like your input about what should be taught for each standard, each grade level. (A standard is a statement that identifies the general knowledge and skills that students should know after several years of schooling.)

Please read each item carefully. Then tell us how important each benchmark (a more specific learning outcome) is for our students with disabilities at that grade level. Circle one of these answers.

VI: Very important
I: Important
PN: Probably not important
DN: Definitely not important

Grade 4.

STANDARD: Understands the history of our local community.

1. Understands changes in community life over time.

VI   I   PN   DN

ADDING LIFE SKILLS TO
THE SPECIAL CURRICULUM

The term *life skills* is used here to mean the processes used in everyday life to solve problems, make decisions, and succeed as a family member, worker, and student. Although Kendall and Marzano (1997) recognize the need for this component in the regular curriculum, it rarely appears in district curricula. And it seems especially useful for students with disabilities. Therefore, the recommendation here is that the special curriculum should emphasize the life skills. Here, in brief, is one process that can be used.

Begin by reviewing the literature on life skills, giving special attention to the recommendations of the state office. Identify the Life Skills standards that you consider useful. Here, for example, is a list (paraphrased from Loyd & Brolin, 1997) of the standards that deal with daily living skills:

♦ Managing money

♦ Maintaining supportive living environments

♦ Maintaining personal health

♦ Developing appropriate personal relationships

♦ Using appropriate behavior while dining, at home and in the community

♦ Buying and maintaining clothing

♦ Participating in leisure activities

♦ Finding your way in the community

The task force would then identify the grade-level benchmarks for each standard. Here, for example, are the middle-grades benchmarks that might be identified for the standard "maintaining personal health":

Grade 6:   Diet and nutrition

Grade 7:   Exercise

Grade 8:   Healthful environments

THE THREE-PART CURRICULUM:
THE INDIVIDUAL CURRICULUM

The third leg is the individual curriculum. The regular curriculum is for all students and is adapted for students with disabilities. The special curriculum is for all students with disabilities who cannot handle the regular curriculum. The individual curriculum is designed for one student only, with the intent to help him or her to achieve a productive life.

The individual curriculum also addresses any special factors that need to be considered for each student. These special factors may include such interventions as behavioral interventions, instruction in Braille, use of assistive technology, provision of special devices, and accommodations for special disabilities. For example, a deaf student might continue to work on this standard: Communicate effectively with American Sign Language. The individual curriculum is developed by analyzing the special needs of one student—needs not addressed by either the regular or special curriculum. The individual curriculum is determined by a systematic evaluation of the student's unique needs.

ASSEMBLING THE COMPONENTS
OF THE WRITTEN CURRICULUM

At this point the task force should be able to develop the components of the written curriculum—the scope and sequence chart and the curriculum guide.

DEVELOPING THE SCOPE
AND SEQUENCE CHART

One scope and sequence chart should be developed for the regular curriculum and one for the special curriculum. A scope and sequence chart, as the term implies, is a large chart that shows the scope of the curriculum by listing the standards down the left side and the sequence, by listing the grades across the top. The benchmarks are noted in each appropriate cell.

Although many school systems do not bother developing a scope and sequence chart, it serves several purposes. It guides the development of the curriculum. It helps special educators and teaching teams see the progression of knowledge and skills across the levels of the curriculum. It provides a useful road map for parents. And it enables all involved to see at a glance the skills and knowledge to be emphasized.

Figure 6.8 shows the form of a scope and sequence chart for grades 1 through 4. Down the left are the standards; across the top are the grades. The benchmarks are noted in each cell, for a particular grade, for each standard.

FIGURE 6.8. EXAMPLE OF SCOPE AND SEQUENCE CHART, SPECIAL CURRICULUM

Standard	Grade			
	1	2	3	4
1. Family life	1. Our families	1. Grandparent families		1. Families long ago
2. Local community	1. Where we live	1. Where grandparents lived	1. Protectors in our community	
3. Democratic values	1. Honesty	1. Respect	1. Freedom	1. Trust
4. Folklore	1. Nursery rhymes	1. Folk tales		1. Myths
5. Discoveries				1. Wheel 2. Fire control 3. Automobile

Throughout this process, the goal of the task force is to develop a scope and sequence chart that is characterized by the following features:

- It specifies no more than ten standards for each subject, Grades K-12.
- For each standard, it specifies no more than four benchmarks for each grade, each standard.
- The placement of benchmarks reflects the developmental capabilities of students with disabilities.
- The placement of benchmarks shows progression from level to level, without excessive repetition.

Note, however, that the grade level designations should be used very flexibly. The teaching team should place each student where he or she belongs developmentally, regardless of the grade.

DEVELOPING THE CURRICULUM GUIDE

The next step in the curriculum process is to use the scope and sequence chart as a basis for developing a useful curriculum guide for each subject included in the curriculum. The goal is to produce a curriculum guide that is teacher friendly. A teacher friendly guide is one that is clear, easy to use, and sharply focused on the essentials. The recommendation here is that each guide should include these elements in the order listed:

- A statement about the importance of special education.
- An explanation of the regular curriculum, organized by levels.
- For each level, a statement of the standards and their benchmarks.
- A similar explanation and description of the special curriculum.
- Guidelines for writing IEPs based on the curriculum guide. (See Figure 6.9, page 102.)
- A synthesis of the research on teaching students with disabilities. (See Chapter 11 for a summary.)

FIGURE 6.9. EXAMPLE OF STANDARDS-BASED IEP

STUDENT: Drew Everett   DATE OF BIRTH: 6/21/90

SCHOOL: Pleasant Elementary   GRADE: 5

PERIOD COVERED: 8/31/00–6/3/01

PRESENT LEVEL OF EDUCATIONAL PERFORMANCE

Drew has a general level of understanding his family's and his grandparents' lives. He is able to present a general overview of his community's history.

ANNUAL GOAL

Drew will understand the people and events significant in the history of the state.

Benchmarks (Short-Term Objectives)	Curriculum Type	Type of Adaptation	Performance Task	Performance Assessment
1. Name one governor of North Carolina and explain why he was important.	Special	*Performance standard	Oral report in small group.	Teacher observation
2. Identify one inventor from North Carolina and name the invention	Special	**Performance assessment	Model of invention	Use of simplified rubric
3. Explain significance of 1999 hurricanes and how they affected the economy.	Regular	***Performance assessment; learning materials.	Poster	Use of simplified rubric

NOTES: * Other students name 3; ** Evaluated with simplified rubric; *** Materials at a 3rd grade level; simplified rubric.

Some districts include the classroom learning objectives. These are the very specific outcomes for each benchmark. Here, for example, are the learning objectives for the Grade 3 benchmark for the "learning to learn" standard:

- ◆ BENCHMARK: Learning from the library.
    1. Showing good behavior in the library.
    2. Taking care of library books.
    3. Using the computerized catalog.
    4. Finding and using encyclopedias in the library.

The recommendation is that the objectives not be included in the curriculum guide. Instead they can be specified in the IEP, thus giving the teacher more flexibility.

Note also that the individual curriculum is not included in the guide, because it is completely individualized. Instead it becomes an important component of the IEP, as explained below.

DEVELOPING IEPs FROM THE THREE PARTS

It should now be a relatively simple matter to use the three parts of the curriculum to write an IEP for each student. The IEP committee should answer these questions in doing so:

- ◆ Which standards and benchmarks from the regular curriculum should be emphasized?
- ◆ How should the regular curriculum be adapted?
- ◆ Which standards and benchmarks from the special curriculum should be emphasized?
- ◆ How can the individual curriculum address special needs not met by the regular or special curriculum?
- ◆ What instructional strategies should be used for the regular, the special, and the individual curriculum?
- ◆ How will student learning be assessed, both formatively and summatively?

Figure 6.9 is one example of an IEP based on these components.

A CONCLUDING NOTE

Students with disabilities deserve the best. A quality curriculum is one major component of excellence in education for students with disabilities.

REFERENCES

Ford, A., Davern, L., & Schnorr, R. (1992). Inclusive education: Making sense of the curriculum. In S. Stainback & W. Stainback (Eds.), *Curriculum considerations in inclusive classrooms* (pp. 37–64). Baltimore: Brookes.

Glatthorn, A. A. (1999). *Performance standards and authentic learning*. Larchmont, NY: Eye on Education.

Kendall, J. S., & Marzano, R. J. (1997). *Content knowledge: A compendium of standards and benchmarks for K–12 education* (2nd ed.). Alexandria, VA: Association of Supervision and Curriculum Development.

Loyd, R. J., & Brolin, D. E. (1997). *Life-centered career education*. Reston, VA: Council for Exceptional Children.

Mastropieri, M.A., & Scroggs, T. E. (1992). Science for students with disabilities. *Review of Educational Research, 62*, 377–411.

Schrag, J. A. (1993). *Organizational , instructional, and curricular strategies to support the implementation of unified, coordinated, and inclusive schools*. Reston, VA: Council for Exceptional Children.

7

USING CURRICULUM STANDARDS AND BENCHMARKS TO DEVELOP LONG-TERM PLANS

With the curriculum guide developed, you should be ready to develop long-term plans for the students with disabilities. A long-term plan shows what you will teach over a single semester or year. Though most teachers do not develop long-term plans, such plans have several advantages. They help make decisions about the focus of units and the time allotted, thus serving as a global view of the term's work. They aid in securing materials in a timely fashion. They assist in designing instruction so that the students have access to the curricula planned for them. They help you communicate with parents about the curriculum. And they serve as the next key step in developing interesting units for your students. This chapter explains one process for developing a long-term calendar for students with disabilities. Other processes may work just as well.

DEVELOP AN APPROPRIATE FORM

Begin the planning process by developing or adapting a long-term planning form. A good form will simplify and organize your decision-making. Figure 7.1 (p. 108) is a form that numerous teachers have used successfully.

Begin by listing the weeks of the school year. In the "Events" column note any event occurring in the nation, state, local community, or school that might affect you and your students. Here are some examples: Martin Luther King's birthday; election day; Halloween; senior prom; class trip; county fair; Rosh Hashanah. Now you are ready to make the substantive decisions.

FIGURE 7.1. EXAMPLE OF LONG-TERM PLANNING CHART

Week	Events	Unit Title	Source	Standard	Benchmarks
10/1–5	Parent Confer-ence	The Rev-olution	Regular Curricu-lum, Adapted	Causes and Events of Revolu-tion	1. Declara-tion of In-depend-ence 2. Events of War
10/8–12		The Rev-olution	Regular, Adapted	Causes and Events of Revolu-tion	3. Major Bat-tles 4. Leaders and Heroes

DECIDE ON THE
NUMBER OF UNITS

With the first two columns completed, your next task is to get the big picture by deciding how many units you will teach. You consider the strengths and limitations of your students. You review the curriculum guide—both the one used for regular students and that used for students with disabilities. You reflect about the time available—about 32 weeks when all the non-instructional time is deducted. You decide you will plan for ap-proximately sixteen two-week units, knowing that some units will be shorter and some longer than that. There is no need to re-cord this decision on the planning form; the number of units will become obvious once you have completed the chart.

In making decisions about the allocation of time, keep in mind two basic principles. First, allot time primarily on the basis of the students' special needs. A student with a learning disabil-ity probably needs more time for reading rather than social studies. Second, most students with disabilities will retain more if they work on in-depth units that provide time for review and remediation. Trying to "cover" too much curriculum territory is dysfunctional for them.

REFLECT ABOUT THE TYPES OF UNITS

Before deciding about unit titles, you should reflect about the types of units you will plan. You have three choices.

Standards focused units are built around a single standard and its benchmarks.

Here is a standards focused unit from geography:

♦ Standard: Knows the location of places, geographic features, and patterns

of the environment.

♦ Benchmark: Grade 3: Knows the location of major cities in North America.

♦ Unit title: Finding Our Cities

Unified units derive their goals from two or more standards and their benchmarks from the same subject. Here is a unified unit from geography:

♦ Standard 3. Understands characteristics and uses of spatial organization.

♦ Benchmark, Grade 3. Knows different methods used to measure distance.

♦ Benchmark, Grade 3. Knows how the technology has affected relationships between locations.

♦ Unit Title: Measuring Distance: Driving Time and Miles Apart

Integrated units include standards from two or more subjects. Here is an example of a unit that integrated geography and language arts:

♦ Standard: Knows the location of places, geographic features, and patterns of the environment. (Geography)

♦ Benchmark: Grade 3: Knows the location of major cities in North America.

♦ Standard: Effectively gathers and uses information for research purposes. (Language arts)

- Benchmark, Grade 3. Uses encyclopedias to gather information for research topics.
- Unit title: Learning about our Big Cities

Standards-focused units are easiest to plan; integrated units, the most difficult. If you decide to plan integrated units, then you would examine the standards and benchmarks from two or more subjects.

CHOOSING UNIT TITLES

The next task is to decide on the unit titles. The unit title should indicate clearly the general topic or overall goal of the unit. In making this decision, you consider several factors. You reflect about the students with disabilities you will be teaching. You review the curriculum guide to note the standards and benchmarks included in the curriculum guide. You confer with the classroom teacher to note the units planned for the regular fifth-grade class and when they will be taught. Here are some examples of unit titles for students with disabilities:

- *English Language Arts:* The Sounds of Poetry
- *Health*: The Food we Need
- *Mathematics:* Working with Triangles
- *Science*: Underneath the Ocean
- *Social Studies:* Families: Now and Then

DETERMINE THE SEQUENCE OF UNITS

The next step is to determine the optimal sequence of the units you have so far identified. Several ways of sequencing are available to you, as follows:

- Chronological

    You sequence by time, from earliest to latest. This time order is typically found in history.
- Student Interest and Ability

    Some teachers like to begin with a high-interest unit to motivate students to take the work seriously; others like to begin with an easy-to-learn unit, to give students a success experience.

♦ Structure and Logic of the Discipline

This method of sequencing organizes units in relation to the conceptual organization of the discipline. This means essentially that the first unit is the most fundamental; then the second grows out of the first and leads to the third. As usually conceptualized by mathematicians, math has a clear linear structure that lends itself to this way of sequencing.

♦ Close-to-Distant

This method of sequencing begins with the near at hand or the most familiar and then moves out in ever-widening circles. Here, for example, is the way elementary social studies is often organized: family, community, state, nation, world.

♦ Holidays

Many elementary teachers structure at least part of their planning so that it is responsive to national holidays. They would use a sequence something like this: October, Columbus and Halloween; November, Thanksgiving and the Pilgrims; December, Hanukkah and Christmas; and so on.

Obviously many teachers would combine two or more sequencing principles. This sequence pattern is an example:

1. Begin with a high interest unit.
2. Use the structure of the discipline for the next five units.
3. Continue with a holiday unit.
4. Move back to the structure of the discipline.

TAKE THE FINAL STEPS

All these decisions should be recorded. Then you would review the plan with the students with disabilities in mind. These questions should be useful in this review.

Does the long-term plan...

- Provide optimal pacing for students with disabilities, ensuring that they have sufficient time to master the content?
- Respond to the special interests and needs of the students?
- Address the standards and benchmarks that are considered essential for students with disabilities?
- Use a sequence that can be communicated to students with disabilities?

8

DEVELOPING PERFORMANCE TASKS FOR STUDENTS WITH DISABILITIES

After you have developed your long-term plans for the term or year, you have two choices about the next step. You can use the long-term schedule to begin the development of units—or you can develop the performance tasks. The recommendation here is to identify the performance tasks and then shape the unit so that your students with disabilities can do well when the assessment is made. This chapter explains the nature of performance tasks and then presents a process for designing a performance task.

UNDERSTAND THE NATURE OF PERFORMANCE TASKS

Performance task is a complex, open-ended problem posed for the students to solve as a means of demonstrating mastery; the performance tasks constitute the bases for the performance assessment. Marzano and Kendall (1996) identify these defining characteristics of a performance task: requires knowledge to be applied to a specific situation, provides necessary guidance and information to complete the task, specifies the learning context (independent, pairs, small groups), and specifies how students will demonstrate their findings or solution.

Some experts in the field use *performance assessment* to mean the same thing. However, it makes sense to differentiate the two terms. To clarify the difference between tasks and assessments, here is an example from an eighth grade language arts unit, shown together with its standard and benchmark:

THE STANDARD: Effectively gathers and uses information for research purposes.

BENCHMARK (Grade 8): Understands the concept of a *likely informant* for obtaining information about a specific topic.

PERFORMANCE TASK: What was life in the United States like in the 1950s? You and your other group members will first choose four likely informants. A likely informant is a person who could help you answer that question. After you have chosen your likely informants, you will then interview them. With this information collected, you will then present a dramatic skit showing what life was like in the 1950s.

PERFORMANCE ASSESSMENT: The evaluators would assess the students' performance on the task, examining such issues as the following:

- Do the students understand the concept of *likely informant?*

- Did the students make a wise choice of informants?

- Was the skit interesting and accurate?

TAKE THE FIRST STEPS: REVIEW STANDARDS, BENCHMARKS, AND UNIT TITLES

With those terms clarified and the long-term plan developed, you are ready to design the first performance task. Obviously there is no right way to do this. The process explained below draws from the extensive literature in the field and the recommendations of teachers who have developed valid tasks. The process should be implemented flexibly. The discussion that follows explains how a fifth-grade team developed a performance task for a cluster of four students with disabilities. The team decided to use the following Health Education standard and its Grade 5 benchmark (paraphrased from Kendall & Marzano, 1997):

STANDARD: Knows how to maintain mental and
physical health.

BENCHMARK (Grade 8): Knows strategies for resisting peer pressure.

First, review the standard and its benchmark. Then check
your earlier decisions about the unit title and the time allocation. Since initially identifying the title and the time, you may
have reconsidered your initial choices. The team working on the
standards and benchmarks noted above have decided to call the
unit "Saying No." They believe they will be able to help the students with disabilities meet the standard and the benchmark in
7 lessons.

Then reflect about the students—their interests, their knowledge, their needs. The team members realize that their students
with disabilities probably have difficulty in resisting peer pressure, because they very much want peer approval. Also consider the related classroom learning objectives. The classroom
learning objectives are the very specific statement of the outcomes desired; they are the components of the benchmark. For
example, the benchmark in the example above might be analyzed into these learning objectives:

♦ Explains "peer pressure."

♦ Understands why some peers put pressure on others to do harmful things.

♦ Demonstrates three strategies for resisting peer
pressure.

DESIGN THE PERFORMANCE TASK

After this reflection, turn to the task itself. Picture the students with disabilities as they work in an inclusive classroom.
Will they work together in a cluster? Will they become part of a
cooperative group? What performance task can be designed
that will require them to access knowledge and apply it in demonstrating their learning?

Brainstorm the performance tasks that might be used. Sus-
pending critical judgment, team members should do some free-
wheeling creative thinking, simply listing all the possibilities.

Here are some of the ideas that the fifth-grade team put on the table:

- ◆ Have students interview the principal.
- ◆ Play a video cassette showing how to handle peer pressure.
- ◆ Discuss what peer pressure is.
- ◆ Ask students to discuss positive peer pressure.
- ◆ Have students do a skit.
- ◆ Have students make an audio- or videotape.

Next, make a preliminary evaluation of the brainstorming results, and combine ideas or select the one that seems most promising. At this stage the team should assess the results of the brainstorming. The assessment here should involve two components: a validity check and a reality check. The validity check answers the central question: "Will this performance task enable students to acquire and use the skills and knowledge embodied in the standards and benchmarks?" If a performance task seems stimulating and motivating but does not relate directly to the standards and benchmarks, then it is seriously flawed. The reality check answers this question: "Will it work in the classroom?" In making the reality check, you should examine such issues as the students' ability to complete the task successfully, student interest in the task, the knowledge resources required, the time the task will take, and the teachability of the task. A more systematic evaluation of the performance task will take place later, as explained below.

Here is the first draft of a performance task that might result from reviewing the brainstorming results in the example:

> You will be part of a group. Your group will present a videotape on peer pressure. Your group will show how to respond when other students tell you to do something that you know is wrong. You then will hold a discussion explaining why students use peer pressure.

Next, make a preliminary evaluation of the first draft and revise as necessary, focusing on these issues. With help, will they be able to perform the task successfully? Does the performance task address the benchmarks and learning objectives? In their preliminary assessment of the first draft, the team realized that the task did not address this objective: Explain peer pressure. They revised accordingly, specifying that the broadcast should also explain the concept of *peer pressure.*

CONDUCT A FORMAL
EVALUATION OF THE TASK

Although the preliminary evaluation can be conducted by the team itself, a more systematic evaluation should involve the supervisor, principal, parents, and other teachers. You should find the criteria listed in Figure 8.1 (p. 120) helpful in this evaluation process. (The following sources were useful in deriving the criteria: Herman, Aschbacher, & Winters, 1992; and Wiggins, 1996.)

A CONCLUDING NOTE

At this point you have completed a crucial step in the entire process. The performance task is essential in developing units and assessing performance.

REFERENCES

Herman, J. L., Aschbacher, P. R., & Winters, L. (1992). *A practical guide to alternative assessment.* Alexandria, VA: Association for Supervision and Curriculum Development.

Kendall, J. S., & Marzano, R. J. (1997). *Content knowledge.* Aurora, CO: Mid-continent Regional Educational Laboratory.

Marzano, R. J., & Kendall, J. S. (1996). *A comprehensive guide to designing standards-based districts, schools, and classrooms.* Alexandria, VA: Association for Supervision and Curriculum Development.

Wiggins, G. (1996). Practicing what we preach in designing authentic assessments? *Educational Leadership, 54* (4), 18–25.

FIGURE 8.1. STANDARDS FOR PERFORMANCE TASKS

Does the Performance Task...

1. Correspond closely and comprehensively with the standard and benchmarks it is designed to assess?
2. Require the students to access prior knowledge, acquire new knowledge, and use that knowledge in completing the task?
3. Require the use of higher thought processes, including creative thinking?
4. Seem real and purposeful, embedded in a meaningful context that seems authentic?
5. Engage the students' interest?
6. Require the students to communicate to classmates and others the processes they used and the results they obtained?
7. Require sustained effort over a significant period of time?
8. Provide the student with options?
9. Seem feasible in the context of schools and classrooms, not requiring inordinate resources or creating undue controversy?
10. Convey a sense of fairness to all, being free of bias?
11. Challenge the students, yet is within their ability to succeed?
12. Provide for both group and individual work, with appropriate accountability?

9

DEVELOPING CURRICULUM UNITS FOR STUDENTS WITH DISABILITIES

An interesting and challenging performance task will provide a sound foundation in designing standards-based units for your students.

UNDERSTAND THE IMPORTANCE OF UNIT PLANNING

Planning units based on performance tasks will help you in your planning and also facilitate student achievement. Several arguments can be advanced for developing units, rather than simply presenting the task to students and focusing on single lessons. The unit emphasizes unified and cohesive elements of the curriculum, not fragmented pieces. The unit is broad enough to encompass systematically the skills needed for the performance assessment. The unit shows your students the relationship of parts. The unit is the best structure for organizing problem-solving activities. And the written unit provides a solid base for your own teaching.

UNDERSTAND HOW TO IMPROVE EXISTING UNITS

Should you always design new units? Though new units will seem fresher and more current, you may wish to save time by modifying existing units, retrofitting some of your or your colleagues' units previously developed.

Suppose, for example, that you had been using with your students a unit on selecting items at the supermarket. In this unit you had taken them to the supermarket to show them how to get the best buy—by reading the supermarket labels on the counters to figure the unit price. They then walked up and down the aisles, noting the unit prices on items you had prese-lected. You assessed their learning by checking their list of unit prices.

How could you improve the unit? You have several choices. First, you can change how they get the information they need. Rather than explaining in the supermarket, where they were easily distracted, you present in the classroom large visuals showing examples of supermarket price labels. Second, you can change the performance task. In the example given, you might decide to explain to students the nutrition pyramid. You would give each student $50 in play money to buy the most nutritious groceries. Finally, you can change the performance assessment. Rather than simply listing unit prices, you would determine if the students chose the most economical and nutritious items.

TAKE THE INITIAL STEPS

When you are ready to design new units, you should find the following process helpful. In this chapter the following ex-ample will be used to illustrate the processes:

STANDARD: Use skills needed for effective living.

BENCHMARK (Grade 8): Shop wisely for basic needs.

PERFORMANCE TASK: Suppose that your group is planning a weekend camping trip. You will all go shopping at the Food Tiger for the food you will need for the weekend. Your group will be given $75 in play money to use at the Food Tiger. Your group will also be given a shopping calculator.

  1. Make a shopping list. Be sure you have listed food that is good for you. Have your teacher check your list.

  2. Go to the supermarket and get a cart.

  3. Start with the first item on your list. Read the big signs to find where the item is on the shelf.

  4. Read the label carefully. Check the unit price. Your teacher will explain *unit price.*

5. If you decide to buy an item, note the price on your list and put a big check mark on the item in the list.

6. Each time you buy an item, add it to your total on the shopping calculator.

7. When you have finished, ask for a cashier named Molly. She will be expecting you. Go to Molly's line. She will check you out and give you a receipt. Use your play money to pay for what you have bought. If you have spent too much, she will ask you to return some of what you have bought.

Review the performance task. Remember that it will serve as the organizing center of the unit. With the task in mind, develop the *unit scenario*. Chapter 8 taught you about the task scenario. The unit scenario is a mental picture of how the unit unfolds. It is a tentative "talk-it-out" description of the key elements of the unit as it will be implemented in the classroom. Here are the questions you should answer in laying out the scenario:

+ How will the unit begin? A good beginning will stimulate student interest and give them an overview of the unit.

+ What knowledge will students need and how will they gain access to it?

+ What group structure will be used—whole class, small group, individual?

+ What steps will students take to complete the performance task?

+ What learning strategy will be taught in the context of the unit? A learning strategy is a mental process useful in solving problems. Here is an example: Use a web diagram to show relationships. Learning strategies (which used to be called "thinking skills") are best taught in the context of solving problems.

+ How will you make a performance assessment?

Those steps need not be taken in order. Remember that the scenario is a tentative mental image. Here is an example of the scenario for the task used above:

> This should be as real as possible. Four of the disabled students in a cluster group. Maybe start with asking them if they shop and how they do it. They'll need to get some knowledge. Maybe have the aide explain unit price, show them how to read the section signs, and use the calculator. Check their shopping lists carefully to be sure they are not buying a lot of junk food. Take them to the supermarket and guide them through the steps. In class the next day help them assess how well they did.

TAKE THE NEXT STEPS

With that scenario in mind, you should now make the following decisions, recording your decisions on the chart shown in Figure 9.1. Figure 9.1 has been partially completed using the example of the shopping unit.

All these decisions can be recorded in a form similar to the one shown in Figure 9.1. Most teachers who have used it report that they have found it to be useful. Down the left side are listed the standard components of an assessment based unit: classroom learning objectives, group structure, knowledge needed and means of access, performance task steps, learning strategy, performance assessment, and resources. Across the top are listed the days of the unit—a 2-week unit has 10 days; a 3-week unit has 15 days. Figure 9.1 shows only the first three days as an example.

A form such as this serves several important functions. It reminds you and your team of the major components you should include. By examining the form with a horizontal perspective, you can see how the individual lessons build upon each other and how knowledge and strategies are developed. By examining the chart from a vertical perspective, you can check the content of the lesson plan for a given day.

FIGURE 9.1. UNIT PLANNING FORM

GRADE: 6–8   DEVELOPER: Marquez

NUMBER OF LESSONS: 5   STUDENTS FOR WHOM IN-
                                             TENDED: Middle school stu-
                                             dents with mild disabilities

STANDARD: Develop life   BENCHMARK: Shopping
   skills

Component	Lesson 1	Lesson 2	Lesson 3
Classroom Learning Objectives	1. Explain why shopping important	1. Explain unit price 2. Explain aisle signs	1. Grouping a random list
Group Structure	Cluster	Cluster	Cluster
Knowledge Access	1. Activate prior knowledge	1. Listen to explanation by aide	1. Listen to teacher explanation
Performance Task Work	1. Gain overview of task		1. Group shopping list
Special Learning Activities		1. Practice reading aisle signs	
Learning Strategies			1. Grouping a random list
Performance Assessment	1. Assess prior knowledge	1. Check knowledge of terms	1. Check grouping
Resources		1. Handout, store layout 2. Aisle signs	1. Handout of sample lists not grouped
Other			
Notes			

1. Identify the classroom learning objectives for each day. As previously explained, the classroom learning objectives are the specific components of the benchmark. List the objectives on the day when they will be emphasized. Each day should have one or more objectives.

2. Indicate the group structure to be used for each day: whole class, heterogeneous groups, cluster group, individual work.

3. The next step in translating the performance task into a unit is to determine what knowledge students will need to complete the task successfully, and how they will gain access to that knowledge. Ample research has demonstrated conclusively that expert problem solvers operate from a deep knowledge of the subject. (See, for example, Leithwood & Steinbach, 1995). You answer this question by reviewing the standards and benchmarks and by analyzing the knowledge demands of the task. In carrying out this critical analysis, make a comprehensive list and then review it, keeping in mind the abilities of the students.

   Here are the results of this review for the shopping task:

   - Unit price
   - Layout of supermarket
   - Use of calculator

In most cases, the knowledge acquisition will occur during the first two or three days of the unit. Note on the chart those days when students will access knowledge.

After you have identified the knowledge needed, you next decide how students will gain access to or acquire that knowledge. Here are some options to consider: listen to teacher, aide, or guest presentation, view video, use computer, learn from trained peers, read text and other print materials, listen to audio cassettes, interview expert, conduct an experiment.

The simplest and most direct means of facilitating access is for you to present the knowledge. Even though "teacher lecture" has been ridiculed as hopelessly old-fashioned, it still can be an effective tool in the hands of an effective teacher. Keep in mind, however, that not all students can learn by listening. Also, varying the means of access will probably enhance student interest.

4. Next you should determine the specific steps that students should take in completing the performance task, once they have acquired the necessary knowledge. You do this through a *task analysis,* asking yourself this question: "If I were the students, what steps would I take in completing the task?" Here is a list for the shopping task:
   - Make a shopping list and have it checked by teacher.
   - Group the final list by kinds of items as classified by the store.
   - Identify location of items.
   - Check unit prices.
   - Check nutrition information.
   - Use calculator to determine running total.

5. The next step is to identify any special learning activities. Many of the other components will imply such activities. This row is a place to call attention to any special learning activities not listed elsewhere.

6. The next step is to identify the *learning strategies* that students will need to master in order to complete the task successfully. As the term is used here, a learning strategy (thinking skill) is a complex mental operation used in solving a problem. Some strategies are subject specific, such as this one for mathematics: In solving a math problem, identify

the knowns. Some can be used in several subjects, such as this one: Organize information by using a matrix.

After reflecting about the time available, what the students already know, and what is absolutely essential for them to know, identify one or two strategies that you would teach in the unit. Experts now agree that such strategies are best taught in the context of real problems to solve, not as isolated skills. For example, in the shopping unit, you would need to teach the strategy of how to categorize a mixed and random list of items.

7. Next you will need to determine both the *formative* and the *summative* assessments you will make. The formative assessments are those you make during the learning process. Here are some of the ways you can make formative assessments: evaluate work samples in progress, observe students at work, administer a written quiz, evaluate homework, conduct a recitation, have students write in journals.

The summative assessment is the performance assessment, as you and the other assessors make a final judgment about student performance.

8. The final step is to note for each day the resources needed—textbook, handout, special guest, software, other media.

PREPARE THE UNIT
FOR EVALUATION

You should now prepare the unit for evaluation and use. Here are the elements of the unit package that are usually included:

- ◆ Identifying information: School district and address, names of developers, date of publication
- ◆ Title of the unit
- ◆ School subject and grade level of intended use

♦ Students for whom the unit was written

♦ Suggested number of lessons

♦ Curriculum standard and benchmarks addressed

♦ A copy of the unit planning form, along with any explanations needed

♦ Performance task, with criteria and rubrics

♦ Form for evaluating the unit

ARRANGE FOR EVALUATION OF THE UNIT

Each unit should undergo several types of evaluation, using the criteria shown in Figure 9.2 (p. 132) or your own set of criteria. First, as you develop and then complete the unit, you and your colleagues should do a formative evaluation, checking periodically to ensure that you are developing quality materials. When you have finished preparing the unit, you should then do a summative evaluation using the same criteria. After making any needed revisions, you should ask teachers who will be using the unit to review and evaluate it, using the criteria and giving you specific suggestions for improving it. You should embody their suggestions in another revision. The real test comes when the students use it. Here the most important criterion is the unit's effectiveness in preparing students to master the performance task. Teachers should supply written feedback on how well the students performed on the task specified.

REFERENCE

Leithwood, K., & Steinbach, R. (1995). *Expert problem solving*. Albany, NY: SUNY Press.

FIGURE 9.2. CRITERIA FOR EVALUATING UNITS

Does the unit...

- Prepare the students to achieve mastery of the performance task?
- Embody the elements of authentic learning?
- Use a realistic time frame?
- In format, organization, and content facilitate teacher use?
- Include all the components specified by the district curriculum office?
- Use language effectively and correctly?

10

MAKING
PERFORMANCE
ASSESSMENTS THAT
MEET THE STANDARDS

Assessments play an important role in the education of students with disabilities. *Screening* is the process of evaluating students to determine who is eligible for special education. *Diagnostic assessment* is a formal process carried out by the team to assess the needs and strengths of an individual student; the diagnostic assessment is a cornerstone of the IEP. This chapter is concerned with classroom assessment as it is connected to student learning, using a model here termed *individualized curriculum based assessment*. The specific standards for such an assessment are shown in Figure 10.1 (p. 136) and serve to organize the rest of this chapter.

USE INDIVIDUALIZED CURRICULUM-BASED ASSESSMENT

Individualized curriculum-based assessment is based on and derives from "curriculum-based assessment," an evaluation model that emphasizes ongoing assessment throughout the learning cycle. (See Fuchs, 1994.) As modified, it is a general approach to student evaluation that has several distinct features. First, it includes all the key stages of the learning cycle: readiness assessment, before the unit begins; formative assessment, as the student proceeds to work through the unit; demonstration assessment, as the student uses a portfolio to demonstrate growth; and summative assessment at the end of the unit based on the previously developed rubrics.

Second, it is individualized, emphasizing individual growth and measuring individual progress. Instead of a standardized measure that provides comparative data about student achievement, it is a learning focused evaluation of one student, compared with the student's prior growth. The question it attempts

FIGURE 10.1. STANDARDS FOR ASSESSMENT

1. The teacher uses *individualized curriculum-based assessment*, choosing evaluation approaches that are sensitive to the student's needs and strengths.

2. The teacher uses *readiness assessment* to determine the additional preparation necessary.

3. The teacher uses *formative assessment* to evaluate the student's progress and to determine if additional scaffolding is needed.

4. The teacher helps the student maintain a *portfolio* to demonstrate learning in progress.

5. The teacher develops and uses *rubrics* to guide the student's self assessment and the teacher's assessment.

6. The teacher uses *performance assessment* that assesses the student's performance in completing the performance task or solving the problem.

7. The teacher uses the results of the assessment to give feedback to the student.

8. The teacher uses data from the performance assessment to adjust teaching and curriculum.

to answer is, "How is Johnny making out, compared with where he had been before?" It does not ask, "Is Johnny doing better than Suzie?" Also, the teacher uses feedback to adjust teaching.

Performance assessments are evaluations of a student's performance or product. They are useful for the student, for the teacher, and for the parent. This chapter will help you use performance assessments as part of the learning cycle.

Finally, individualized curriculum-based assessment uses a variety of measures to track progress: observation, interviews, written and oral quizzes, assessment of work samples. The decision as to which type of assessment measure is used is made on the basis of the student needs and strengths and the efficacy of the measure. Thus, if a student has an attention deficit disorder, the teacher would be wise to assess the student in several short sessions, rather than in one long session.

USE READINESS ASSESSMENT AT THE START OF THE UNIT

At the start of the unit you should use diagnostic assessment to determine if the students have the knowledge and skills necessary for success. Diagnostic assessment for students with disabilities takes many forms.

♦ Oral questions provide an opportunity to assess both experiential and school knowledge. "Do any of you recycle newspapers at home?"

♦ Questions that require a written response often help the student call into awareness what was only dimly sensed. "In your notebook, write what you think *recycle* means."

♦ Written quizzes without the pressure of time give the students with disabilities a chance to think about a question before answering. "Name three products that can be made from old aluminum cans."

♦ Observing students at work can provide some helpful clues. If you see students looking confused, going off task, or showing signs of boredom, you can probe for the causes. "Jon, you look confused. Are you mixed up about something?" These diagnostic measures should indicate to you whether the students need additional teaching before they start the unit.

USE FORMATIVE ASSESSMENT TO EVALUATE PROGRESS

Formative assessments take place as student learning occurs. Observing students at work is probably the best way to make formative assessments of students with disabilities. Here are some issues to consider as you observe students with disabilities at work:

♦ Who is leading the group?

♦ Who is not contributing?

- How are the students resolving differences?
- How much has been accomplished?
- What misunderstandings are being revealed?
- In a heterogeneous group, how are students with disabilities being accepted?

In the formative assessment process, provide corrective feedback and scaffolding, rather than simply ignoring the problem. Scaffolding is the support provided to help the student stretch his or her cognitive reach. You can provide scaffolding in several ways: give oral hints, provide a model of the product desired, write cue cards that remind students of the key points, use metaphors and analogies that the student will recognize. Here is an example of scaffolding for the concept *recycle:*

> Here is an aluminum can of soda. When you are finished with it, you can throw it away into this trash can. Or you can throw it into this special can. This special can will be collected and made into a new can. That is called recycling. The old can comes around again as a new can. Think of a bicycle wheel that turns around again and again.

USE THE PORTFOLIO TO
DEMONSTRATE LEARNING IN PROGRESS

The portfolio is a collection of student work samples used to demonstrate and exemplify accomplishment. It has several audiences: the student, the teacher, and the parent. Teachers who have used portfolios successfully offer these suggestions. First, structure the portfolio carefully so that students know what to include and how to organize the contents. Some teachers have found this general organization effective: the first part of the notebook belongs to the students, which they use as they wish, drawing pictures, writing poems, writing letters, and making notes. This section is called "My Personal Portfolio." Students should be cautioned not to include anything that they wish to keep confidential, because it is difficult to maintain portfolio confidentiality.

The second part of the portfolio is called "My Class Portfolio," and is organized as the teacher directs. There are no strict rules here; simply remember that the primary purpose is to document and exhibit what has been learned. Some teachers have found the following organization helpful.

1. Words I Have Learned

   The students list new words and their meaning, as the students understand the words.

2. Tests I Have Taken

   This includes the major tests the student has taken, with any corrections made later.

3. Problems I Have Solved

   The examples of problems solved will include problems from all the subjects the student has taken, not only mathematics.

4. Books I Have Read

   The student writes a one-sentence summary and a short comment about the book.

5. Projects I Am Working On

   This section should include work-in-progress. It is important in this section to include the first draft of an essay or letter and the final copy.

In using the portfolio with students with disabilities, teachers should emphasize its positive aspects, rather than seeing it as one more item to grade. Help the student feel a sense of pride in documenting what has been learned.

USE RUBRICS TO GUIDE STUDENT AND TEACHER ASSESSMENT

Rubrics are scoring guides, used to help students make a self-assessment and then improve their work, and used also to assist teachers in scoring student work and giving students feedback. Using rubrics for students with disabilities raises very complex and difficult issues about the evaluation of such students. The following recommendations have been derived from a relatively small body of research on this issue and thus need careful examination by special educators and regular teachers. (An excellent source for a general discussion of rubrics is Wiggins, 1998, although there is no discussion of rubrics and students with disabilities; see also Mitchell & Willis, 1995)

Begin with a holistic scoring guide developed especially for students with disabilities. Developing rubrics for students without disabilities is a complex problem requiring special abilities and knowledge. Developing them for students with disabilities is even more complex, best undertaken with a team approach. The team itself should start by developing a simple holistic rubric for a frequently assigned task. A holistic rubric gives a single score based on a general impression. A sample holistic rubric for the employment interview is shown in Figure 10.2.

The sample rubric shown in Figure 10.2 has three elements: the *scale*, the number and label assigned to the levels of performance; the *descriptors*, which identify the characteristics of each level; and the *standard*, the level of performance considered acceptable. In this example the teachers decided that a rating of 4 or 5 on the scale would be acceptable for students with disabilities. And rather than using terms such as "does not meet standard" or "unsatisfactory," they simply indicate to the student that remediation is necessary. Though the holistic rubric is relatively simple to construct and use, it has been criticized for not being sufficiently specific.

Develop an analytic rubric when competence has been achieved. After developing a few satisfactory holistic rubrics, the team should then attempt an analytic rubric. An analytic rubric, as Wiggins explains, identifies each major trait, which then has its own rubric. A sample analytic rubric is shown in Figure 10.3 (p. 142). The rubric was designed for use with high school students with disabilities; the performance task was to write a personal narrative involving a conflict.

FIGURE 10.2. SAMPLE HOLISTIC RUBRIC:
EMPLOYMENT INTERVIEW

Scale	Descriptors
5: Excellent	The student is dressed in a proper way. The student seems neat and clean. The student is polite. The student speaks clearly and correctly. The student answers questions fully. The student asks good questions. The student thanks the interviewer at the end.
4: Very good	The student has only one or two minor problems with dress and appearance. The student is polite most of the time. The student speaks clearly with only one or two errors. The student answers most questions fully. The student forgets to ask about one important issue. The student thanks the interviewer briefly.
1–3: Needs more work	The student does not make a good impression in appearance. The student seems rude at times. The student does not answer questions fully. The student forgets to thank the interviewer.

The teaching team began by rereading some excellent narratives that had been written by previous students with a disability. Those careful re-readings helped them identify the *criteria* that are important in such stories. The criteria are the specific elements that will be judged. For each criterion they then identified the descriptors. Next they determined the rating scale to be used. Their final task was to agree on the standard to be used for this performance task.

FIGURE 10.3. ANALYTIC RUBRIC: PERSONAL NARRATIVE

Characters

4   Characters are described clearly and fully, with major characteristics noted. The descriptions enable the reader to picture all the characters clearly. Characters seem interesting to the readers.

3   Characters are described briefly but it seems difficult to imagine them. One character seems vague.

2–1   Characters are named but not described.

Plot

4   Plot has conflict at the center. Events are told in chronological order. Plot focuses on key actions.

3   Plot has some conflict. Plot presents events in chronological order but does not focus on key actions.

2–1   Plot seems confusing, with little conflict. Events seem out of order.

Setting

4   Setting is fully described with vivid images.

3   Setting is described briefly.

2–1   Setting identified but not described or setting is lacking.

Dialog

4   Dialog is used extensively and effectively. Dialog seems natural.

3   Some dialog is used. Some sounds stilted.

2–1   Dialog is used sparingly or not at all. When used, it seems unnatural.

USE PERFORMANCE ASSESSMENT
TO EVALUATE ACHIEVEMENT

With the rubrics in hand, the teacher can then use performance assessment to assess the student's performance of the task. Thus, performance assessment would typically take place at the conclusion of the unit. The student would demonstrate how he or she has accomplished the goals of the unit and the teacher would evaluate the demonstration. A student with a disability might use one of several methods of demonstrating learning, depending on the unit goal and the nature of the disability.

Here are some of the ways that students with disabilities could demonstrate their learning:

- ◆ Making a sound recording.

    The student makes an audiotape of an interview he/she has conducted.

- ◆ Making a videotape.

    The student makes a videotape of his/her visit to the fire house.

- ◆ Making a live presentation or demonstration.

    The student demonstrates how a plant was grown.

- ◆ Exhibiting a project that has been completed.

    The student exhibits a birdhouse he/she has made.

- ◆ Writing a report.

    The student writes a report on his/her ancestors.

- ◆ Showing the solution to a problem and the work used to solve the problem.

    The student solves a math problem and explains how the problem was solved.

- ◆ Keeping a journal.

    The student keeps a journal about his/her experiences in working a part-time job.

The teacher could use the rubrics to provide feedback to the student, as suggested in Figure 10.4 (p. 144). In making assess-

---

FIGURE 10.4. ASSESSING PERFORMANCE
USING ANALYTIC RUBRIC: PERSONAL NARRATIVE

Characters

4   Characters are described clearly and fully, with major characteristics noted. The descriptions enable the reader to picture all the characters clearly. Characters seem interesting to the readers.

3   Characters are described briefly but it seems difficult to imagine them. One character seems vague.

2–1   Characters are named but not described.

Plot

4   Plot has conflict at the center. Events are told in chronological order. Plot focuses on key actions.

3   Plot has some conflict. Plot presents events in chronological order but does not focus on key actions.

2–1   Plot seems confusing, with little conflict. Events seem out of order.

Setting

4   Setting is fully described with vivid images.

3   Setting is described briefly,

2–1   Setting identified but not described or setting is lacking.

Dialog

4   Dialog is used extensively and effectively. Dialog seems natural.

3   Some dialog is used. Some sounds stilted.

2–1   Dialog is used sparingly or not at all. When used, it seems unnatural.

YOUR SPECIAL STRENGTH: You made very good use of dialog. You have a good ear for the way people talk.

WE WILL DO SOME WORK WITH YOU: We will work together on making the setting clearer. That will make your story even better.

---

ment and giving feedback, keep in mind the basic principle: for all students the primary purpose of assessment is to improve learning. (Wiggins, 1998). This is especially true with students with disabilities (Fuchs, 1994). These students want to do their best; they are not involved in a competitive race with students who are not disabled. This basic guideline implies other principles. Do not give these students grades. Be sure to call attention to what they do well. Be specific about accomplishments and deficiencies. And specify what will be done to help the student overcome any deficiencies.

Use Assessment Data to Make Adjustments

If a student with a disability shows one or more deficiencies, the teacher should use the occasion to make adjustments in teaching or in the curriculum. Suggesting this is not intended to blame the teacher; rather, it simply recognizes the fact that the teacher can control the instructional processes and the curriculum—but cannot control the student's learning. Here the teacher needs to be a problem solver, analyzing what teacher-controlled factors might have contributed to the deficiency and what kind of adjustments are needed. The following list notes the most common causes for insufficient achievement and the adjustments needed:

- Pace of instruction was inappropriate.

    Slow down the pace.

- Method of teaching was ineffective.

    Use a method that compensates for the student's disability and is responsive to learning style.

- Tensions existed between teacher and student.

    Resolve the tensions or use a peer or an adult tutor.

- Concepts were not understood by student.

    Use concrete materials and more examples.

- Task was unclear or inappropriate.

  Give simpler directions, repeating key parts. Choose a performance task more in keeping with student's ability.

- Teacher was not aware of student's difficulties in completing the task.

  Increase the use of formative assessments.

- Student lacked requisite knowledge for completing the task.

  Provide knowledge needed.

- Student did not connect with content.

  Help the student find meaning and purpose in the curriculum.

REFERENCES

Fuchs, L. S. (1994). *Connecting performance assessment to instruction*. Reston, VA: Council for Exceptional Children.

Mitchell, R., & Willis, M. (1995). *Learning in overdrive*. Golden, CO: North American Press.

Paulsen, K. J. (1997). Curriculum-based measurement. *Intervention in School and Clinic, 32*, 162–167.

Wiggins, G. (1998). *Educative assessment*. San Francisco: Jossey-Bass.

11

USING STANDARDS TO IMPROVE TEACHING AND LEARNING

This chapter provides effective strategies that will help you improve your teaching and foster the learning of all students. Keep in mind, however, that your teaching is only one element of dynamic learning. As noted throughout this work, other factors influence learning, such as the school culture, the classroom climate, and the curriculum. This chapter first examines general models that have been shown to be effective. It then notes specific strategies that work with students with disabilities. The chapter also explains a decision-making process and closes by deriving the standards for instruction from the previous analyses.

GENERAL MODELS

Several general models of teaching students with disabilities have been advocated. The following review describes those that have proved to be effective..

MATCHING LEARNING STYLES

Several experts in special education recommend the practice of accommodating the learning style of students with a disability (McGregor & Vogelsberg, 1998). The term "learning style" refers to the way the brain perceives and processes what it needs to learn (Dunn, 1996; Winebrenner, 1996). Students with disabilities seem to learn best when their learning style matches the teaching style of their instructors. Thus, if a student with a disability learns best by listening, he or she will learn the most when the teacher makes brief oral presentations. To make learning happen, the teacher must connect learning to a pattern the brain already recognizes. Equally important, the learning environment should be one in which the student feels comfortable.

Some learning styles models are based on three components of style—cognition (how the learner perceives and applies knowledge), conceptualization (how a learner thinks), and affect (how the learner feels). Others focus on a sensory perspective, identifying three styles: auditory, visual, and tactile-kinesthetic. Auditory learners learn by listening and are logical, analytical, sequential thinkers. Because their learning needs are generally met in the classroom, they are often considered to be "good students." Visual learners learn by seeing and must get a "picture in their brain" in order to understand what they need to learn. They are usually global thinkers. Tactile-kinesthetic students learn by hands-on experience and movement. Many ADHD students are tactile-kinesthetic learners whose hyperactive behaviors could be diminished if their learning tasks allowed them hands-on activities (Winebrenner, 1996).

All babies are born with a predominant tactile-kinesthetic learning style. Babies learn by doing—by touching everything that they can get their hands onto. Success in most school tasks requires children to make the transition from tactile-kinesthetic to auditory-analytical. According to some experts, the brain of the girl is ready to make that transition at about the age of six, whereas the brain of the boy may not be ready for that transition until as late as eight or nine years old (Carbo, Dunn, & Dunn, 1986).

Learning style research also indicates that between 30 to 35 percent of students in a typical classroom are visual learners. Approximately 15 to 30 percent are probably tactile-kinesthetic learners. As teachers design learning activities in their classrooms, it is necessary to remember that all students should be involved in choosing learning conditions that lead to their greatest productivity (Winebrenner, 1996).

Though learning style theory seems to be useful, some critics are not impressed. A summary of the research on the effectiveness of adapting teaching to the preferred learning styles of Native Americans concludes that such accommodation is not effective (Kleinfeld & Nelson, 1991). Other critics have noted these reservations about the studies supporting accommodation: they are poorly designed and susceptible to researcher's bias, the definitions of *learning style* are so inconsistent that it is difficult to synthesize results, and accommodation is not theoretically desirable. (See Glatthorn, 1999.)

Given the inconsistency of these perspectives, two practical guidelines make sense:

1. Use a variety of teaching/learning strategies in every instructional session.
2. If a student with a disability seems not to be learning in one modality, find another.

MULTIPLE INTELLIGENCES MODELS

This model proposes that all people have multiple intelligences. Perhaps the best known is Gardner's "MI" or "Multiple Intelligences" approach. Gardner (1995) believes that there are eight intelligences: linguistic, spatial, logical-mathematical, kinesthetic, musical, interpersonal, intrapersonal, naturalist. This approach would seem to be very useful in structuring the curriculum and using teaching learning activities. Using it in the curriculum would mean that students with disabilities would have a much broader curriculum; the existing curriculum is too narrow, emphasizing only the linguistic, the logical-mathematical, and the naturalist.

Also, if a student with a disability is strong in a given intelligence (such as the spatial one), the teacher would use strategies, such as visual graphics, which capitalize on that strength. (For a review of Gardner's present views, see Checkley, 1997.)

COOPERATIVE LEARNING MODELS

According to Johnson & Johnson (1990), cooperative learning "is the instructional use of small groups so that students work together to maximize their own and one another's learning" (p. 69). Cooperative learning contrasts with competitive and highly individualistic learning. Cooperative learning groups can be composed of small groups of students or a pair of students working together (Hoover & Patton, 1997). The students are responsible not only for their own learning, but the learning of other members of their group. They are also responsible for exhibiting certain social behaviors with their peers. The role of the teacher shifts from presenter of information to a facilitator of learning. The teacher can also adapt lesson requirements for individual students, varying the performance, standard, the pace of learning, and the amount of material to be learned, depending on the needs of the student (Stainback & Stainback, 1992).

Roy (1990) identifies several common elements of cooperative learning:

- Positive interdependence

  This occurs when each student in the cooperative group feels a sense of mutual goals and rewards. Each student understands that all members must complete their task in order to get credit for the work.

- Individual accountability

  There is an assessment of each student's mastery level as well as those of the cooperative group. Cooperative learning does not excuse the individual learner from participating and achieving the objectives.

- Opportunities for interactions

  Students are encouraged to assist others in learning the material. They are encouraged to exchange ideas, provide feedback to one another, encourage student efforts, and support one another's involvement. These interactions strengthen the idea of sharing in a cooperative manner.

- Interpersonal training

  This prepares students for successful interactions in cooperative learning teams. Teachers assist students with communication, conflict management, decision making, leadership, and group process skills. Students with disabilities may need extra help in this area. The success of cooperative learning groups depends on the teacher's ability to prepare students in how teams should function.

- Group processing

This gives the teacher and the student the opportunity to determine how well the group functioned relative to specific tasks. Cooperative team members discuss individual contributions to the group, ways to improve, and recommendations for future cooperative team efforts.

According to Slavin (1991), cooperative learning is effective in enhancing student achievement in all major subject areas, in all grade levels, and with all levels of ability. Inclusive cooperative learning is important when children in the classroom come from different backgrounds and have a wide range of abilities. Successful inclusion of students with disabilities requires a collaborative effort. Students with disabilities can play a valuable role in the classroom but only when the class actively works to accept and include them. Cooperative learning actively promotes care and respect for each other (Hill & Hill, 1990). Johnson and Johnson (1990) state that cooperative learning is effective in helping students learn basic facts, understand concepts, solve problems, and use higher order thinking skills.

TECHNOLOGY-ASSISTED MODELS

Though all learners can profit from the appropriate use of technology, students with disabilities seem to profit most of all. Some experts report that the effective use of technology in the special classroom narrows the gap between potential and performance, especially for students who struggle to achieve (Winebrenner, 1996).

The uses of technology in the classroom can be divided into two types: instructional and assistive (McDonnell, McLaughlin, & Morrison, 1997).

INSTRUCTIONAL TECHNOLOGY

Four instructional uses can be identified. Some software programs provide *tutorial* services, chiefly drill-and-practice exercises, perhaps the most common use. *Exploratory* software enables the student with a disability to explore topics by browsing in several data bases. If guided appropriately, exploratory programs can pique the curiosity of students with disabilities. Some software programs focus on the *communication* function, facilitating student communication with other students, with friends, and with organizations. *Productive* uses such as word-processing and media development emphasize the use of the computer as a creative tool.

The research on instructional uses is judged to be "equivocal," according some reviewers (McDonnell, McLaughlin, & Morrison, 1997, p. 132). As the same reviewers note, the computer is only a tool for delivering instruction: some tools are of excellent quality, some are only mediocre.

ASSISTIVE TECHNOLOGY

Assistive technology can be defined as technology that assists people with physical or sensory limitations. It includes devices that enable users to communicate, carry out everyday tasks, and learn better. According to McDonnell, McLaughlin, and Morrison, assistive technology has produced "dramatic benefits" for those with disabilities (p. 130).

It is important to remember that technology is not a "cure" for a disability, rather it is a tool for everyone in society. Technology can help remove barriers so that all children can be successful in the classroom

PEER TUTORING MODELS

Peer tutoring has proved to be beneficial for both tutees and tutors. (See Gartner & Lipsky, 1990.) For those being tutored, it provides additional time, offers the benefits of individual attention, and facilitates active learning. For the tutor, it is an effective demonstration of the old maxim: "If you really want to learn something, teach it to someone else." In addition to this cognitive benefit, the tutor also gains self-confidence, improves in social skills, and increases his or her self-esteem.

The research suggests that the following features characterize the most effective peer tutoring programs:

- The program is highly structured, with respect to the schedule, the process, and the evaluation.
- Tutors are screened and carefully selected.

♦ Tutors are trained in the specific skills needed to tutor effectively.

♦ Quality materials are used.

Not all students with disabilities can profit from tutoring. However, its general effectiveness has been clearly demonstrated.

DIRECT INSTRUCTION MODELS

The evidence suggests that for almost all students with disabilities, the direct instruction model is effective—for certain types of learning (Epps & Tindal, 1987). Though there have been many formulations of this model, in general it is characterized by these features:

♦ The teacher helps students connect with the topic to be studied.

♦ The teacher clearly specifies the objectives of the lesson.

♦ The teacher explains concepts and skills clearly.

♦ The teacher provides positive and negative examples.

♦ The teacher conducts the lesson at a fairly rapid pace.

♦ The teacher ensures that all students are involved in responding.

♦ The teacher makes frequent assessments of student learning and provides appropriate feedback.

♦ The teacher summarizes and reviews.

Some authors call this model "intensive instruction," which has four key features: achieving a high rate of student responding, matching learning processes with students' cognitive development, using instructional cues, and providing detailed feedback. (See McDonnell, McLaughlin, & Morison, 1997.)

Critics have noted that direct instruction maximizes the role of the teacher as a presenter and minimizes the role of the student as an inquirer. Defenders respond by citing the supporting research.

CONSTRUCTIVIST MODELS

Constructivist models of teaching are based on research in cognitive psychology. Though there are minor differences in how this model is conceptualized, most teaching that uses this approach is characterized by the following features.

- ◆ Each student is a meaning maker, who constructs his or her knowledge. Therefore, the role of the teacher is to facilitate this meaning making.
- ◆ The student will learn best by solving open-ended complex problems. (In Chapter 8, these are identified as *performance tasks*).
- ◆ In solving those problems, the students will apply generative knowledge—knowledge that is used, rather than being inert.
- ◆ In solving those problems, the student should acquire the necessary learning strategies (or thinking skills). These strategies and skills are best learned in the context of solving problems, not in isolation.
- ◆ In much of the problem solving, the students will work together in small cooperative groups.
- ◆ The student's achievement is assessed by a performance assessment, an evaluation of the student's performance in solving the problem. (See Chapter 10.)

Some experts in special education question a few of these principles as they might apply in the teaching of students with disabilities. McDonnell, McLaughlin, and Morison (1997) raise three objections: constructivism minimizes the role of the teacher as a presenter of knowledge and guide of learning; constructivism does not give sufficient attention to the teaching of discrete skills; and constructivism underestimates the importance of a skill hierarchy.

Despite these reservations, the authors of this work believe that teachers of students with disabilities should test out these principles in real classroom settings. In doing so, they can take cognizance of the reservations noted above: vary the role of the teacher as necessary, teach discrete skills as needed, and base the instruction on a hierarchy of skills as needed.

Specific Strategies

In addition to these general models, there are several specific teaching/learning strategies that are very effective with students with disabilities.

♦ Maintaining a focus on the individual student, rather than the class as a whole

Assess the needs and strengths of each student with a disability to determine the next phase of the learning process.

♦ Providing skill-based instruction

Though several learning theorists scoff at the teaching of what they call "fragmented skills," there is evidence that many students with disabilities profit from the explicit teaching of specific skills. Use a problem solving process to determine what each student with a disability needs.

♦ Providing scaffolding with new or difficult tasks

Scaffolding is giving learners cues, hints, and structure. The term is a metaphor that suggests the image of a scaffold that enables workers to reach high places; it is then removed when it is no longer needed. Here are some examples of scaffolding in learning: making a large cue card that reminds students of key steps, giving the student worked out examples, solving problems together, and responding to students' writing by asking questions that help them revise.

♦ Enabling students with disabilities to proceed at their own pace

The pace of learning is a critical component of the learning process. Many special educators have found it effective to help students set a time for completing the task, thus also increasing their independence.

♦ Using small groups as a learning structure

In addition to being the primary structure of cooperative learning, the small group can be effective for students with disabilities in other ways: giving each other feedback on work products, discussing issues, solving problems together, and helping each other. Both heterogeneous and homogeneous groups can be effective. In either case, students with disabilities will need to be taught the skills of effective group participation.

USING A PROBLEM-SOLVING APPROACH

The previous discussions have highlighted the general models and the specific interventions that seem effective with students with disabilities. However, rather than using that knowledge to find the "best" intervention, it makes more sense for the teaching team to use a problem-solving process to design an intervention that would help that individual student. The problem-solving process described below is a mix of several problem solving approaches that teaching teams have found effective.

The following example is used throughout to illustrate each step:

> Robert is a 14-year-old student with a disability who has been identified as mildly retarded mentally. He and his mother seem especially close; long ago she accepted the fact that her son was mentally retarded. His father, who is a research scientist, still doubts that his son is retarded, blaming the school for not accommodating his son's learning style.
>
> The aide, Ms. Wilkins, has asked for the meeting, noting her concern that Robert no longer seems interested in doing math.

DESCRIBE THE BEHAVIOR

The first step is for the educator who knows the student best to describe the behavior objectively and specifically. Rather than using labels or blaming, the presenter gives an objective description of the behavior that suggests that a problem exists. Here is how the teacher aide describes Robert's behavior:

> Robert complains about math. "I don't see the point." He often notes that he can't do math. "I was never good with numbers." When I try to explain a process, he seems to be inattentive and stares off into the distance. When he works on problems, he does only a few and then gives up.

Then others who have knowledge of his present behavior describe what they have observed. It would be especially important to get the parent's perspective. Note that there is no attempt to make a quick diagnosis or solution, such as "His father needs to be more involved with Robert."

ANALYZE THE LIKELY CAUSES

The second phase is to infer from the behavior what are the likely causes. A dialogic process is recommended here. Each person has an opportunity to present his or her analysis, while the others listen actively and constructively. Differences are not personalized but are offered in a constructive manner. Here is an example.

Teacher: I think his problem is nutritional.

Mother: Could you say some more about that?

Teacher: He always seem to be snacking.

Mother: I don't often see that at home. He seems to be afraid of having to compete with his father.

REVIEW THE KNOWLEDGE BASE

One person on the team assumes responsibility for building the knowledge base. Two components are important here: summarizing the research and discerning the experiential knowledge of participants. Because this can be a time-consuming process, the team should rotate this responsibility. The review of the research can be accomplished by using one of the search engines to access ERIC and other sources on the Internet.

The analysis of the experiential knowledge can be accomplished by asking each participant to describe what he or she has learned by working with students similar to Robert. Here is an example of this stage:

> Special educator: The research indicates that low motivation is one symptom of what the experts call "failure avoidance." Failure avoidance is using strategies to avoid failure. The theory is that unmotivated students are actually feeling insecure, doubting their ability. So rather than risking failure and being embarrassed, these students don't even try.

> Classroom teacher: That makes a lot of sense to me. I have known several students with disabilities who seemed to be failure avoiders. I found that just helping them succeed increased their motivation.

OFFERING AND EVALUATING SOLUTIONS

In this stage, creativity is encouraged and negativity is discouraged. Each person in a "round robin" process offers one solution that uses the causal analysis and knowledge base to offer a solution likely to be effective. Their suggestions are listed on the board. Each person then ballots, giving four votes to his or her first choice and two votes to the second choice.

The leader then helps the group evaluate the solutions offered, using two criteria: (a) Is likely to be effective; and (b) Is feasible. The group may decide to combine solutions, as in the following:

> We will ask his father to talk to the whole class about how he uses math. We also will use peer tutoring to help Robert achieve success.

Of course, teams are encouraged to be flexible in using this process, making their own modifications that reflect their special context.

USING STANDARDS FOR TEACHING

From an analysis of both the general models of teaching/ learning and the specific strategies, the standards shown in Figure 11.1 have been derived. Though they are based on sound research, they have not been rigorously tested for validity. Therefore they should not be used to evaluate teachers. Instead they can be used as a basis for staff development, peer coaching, and self-directed goal setting.

FIGURE 11.1. STANDARDS FOR TEACHING

The teacher of students with disabilities...

♦ Maintains a focus on the learning of the individual student.

♦ Makes appropriate accommodation to the needs and learning styles of the individual student.

♦ Uses cooperative learning as one of the primary classroom structures.

♦ Uses technology for a variety of functions.

♦ Makes effective use of peers as tutors.

♦ Uses direct instruction to assist the student with a disability in learning from skill-based instruction.

♦ Provides support and scaffolding when deemed necessary.

♦ Challenges the individual student to solve open-ended problems at an appropriate level of difficulty.

REFERENCES

Carbo, M., Dunn, R. & Dunn, K. (1986). *Teaching students to read through their individual learning styles.* Englewood Cliffs, NJ: Prentice-Hall.

Checkley, K. (1997). The first seven...and the eighth: a conversation with Howard Gardner. *Educational Leadership, 55* (1), pp. 8–13.

Dunn, R. (1996). *How to implement and supervise a learning style program.* Alexandria, VA: Association for Supervision and Curriculum Development.

Epps, S., & Tindal, G. (1987). The effectiveness of differential programming in serving students with mild handicaps. In M. C. Wang, M. C. Reynolds, & H. J. Walberg (Eds.), *Handbook of special education: Research and practice* (Vol. 1) (pp. 213–250). New York: Pergamon.

Gardner, H. (1995). Reflections on multiple intelligences: Myths and messages. *Phi Delta Kappan, 77* (3), 206–209.

Gartner, A., & Lipsky, D. K. (1990). Students as instructional agents. In W. Stainback & S. Stainback (Eds.), *Support networks for inclusive schooling* (pp. 81–94). Baltimore: Brooke.

Glatthorn, A. A. (1999). *Learning styles: A critique.* Greenville, NC: East Carolina University.

Hill, S., & Hill, T. (1990). *The collaborative classroom: A guide to cooperative learning.* Portsmouth, NH: Heinemann.

Hoover, J. J., & Patton, J. R. (1997). *Curriculum adaptations for students with learning and behavior problems: Principles and practices.* Dallas, TX: Pro-Ed.

Johnson, D. W., & Johnson, R. T. (1990). What is cooperative learning? In M. Brubacher, R. Payne, & K. Rickett (Eds.), *Perspectives on small group learning* (pp. 1–30). Toronto, Canada: Rubicon.

Kleinfeld, J., & Nelson, P. (1991). Adapting instruction to Native Americans learn styles. *Journal of Cross-Cultural Psychology, 22,* 273–282.

McDonnell, L. M., McLaughlin, M. J., & Morrison, P.M. (Eds.). (1997). *Educating one and all.* Washington, DC: National Academy Press.

McGregor, G., & Vogelsberg, R. T. (1998). *Inclusive schooling practices: Pedagogical and research foundations.* Baltimore: Brooke.

Roy, P. A. (1990). *Cooperative learning: Students learn together.* Richfield, MN: Author.

Slavin, R. E. (1991) Synthesis of research on cooperative learning. In R. E. Slavin (Ed.), *Cooperative learning and the collabora-*

tive school (pp. 82–89). Alexandria, VA: Association for Supervision and Curriculum Development.

Stainback, S., & Stainback, W. (1992). *Curriculum considerations in inclusive classrooms: Facilitating learning for all students.* Baltimore: Brookes.

Winebrenner, S. (1996). *Teaching kids with learning difficulties in the regular classroom.* Minnesota: Free Spirit Publishing.

PART IV

THE FACILITATING COMPONENTS

12

DEVELOPING AND IMPLEMENTING STANDARDS-BASED IEPS

The individualized education program (IEP) is the blueprint for the delivery of services to students with disabilities. As discussed in Chapter 5, there are certain constraints that must be adhered to in developing the IEP. However, the intent of the IEP is to protect the student and to guarantee the student an appropriate education in the least restrictive setting possible.

This chapter explains the process of developing an IEP, keeping in mind the constraints, and at the same time incorporating the concept of the three-part curriculum (see Chapter 6). The IEP is a yearly plan. Once developed, it can be amended at any time by the IEP committee, of which the parent is always a member.

USING PREVIOUS DECISIONS IN DEVELOPING AN IEP

The intent of the IDEA Amendment of 1997 is to focus on the general curriculum and how the student's disability affects his or her involvement and progress in the general curriculum (IDEA, 1997). Therefore in the development of the IEP, the general or regular or curriculum must first be examined. For purposes of IEP development the format shown in Figure 12.1 (p. 170) is used.

FIGURE 12.1. FORMAT FOR STANDARDS-BASED IEP

I. Student: _____   DOB: _____

School: _____   Grade: _____   From: _____   To: _____

II. Present Level of Educational Performance:

III. Annual Goal:

Benchmark Objective	Curriculum Type	Adaptation	Performance Task	Performance Assessment

Consider this standard for a sixth-grade communications skills classroom: Read literary materials with complex characters, settings, and events with teacher support. Mary is a severely visually impaired student enrolled in a regular classroom setting. She is in the sixth grade. The IEP committee has determined that Mary is able to master the standards of the regular curriculum, though at the same time needing some specific goals that apply to her visual impairment. Therefore, she requires the use of adaptive technology to enable her to progress in the regular curriculum. These technological aids include Braille textbooks, software that converts regular text to Braille, a Braille keyboard, a Braille printer, and a cane. A sample of her IEP for her regular curriculum is shown in Figure 12.2.

Figure 12.2. Standards-Based IEP

I. Student: <u>Mary Smith</u>　　　　　DOB: <u>11-09-87</u>

School:　　　　　　Grade:　From:　　To:
　<u>Newton Elementary</u>　<u>6</u>　　<u>6/2/99</u>　　<u>6/1/2000</u>

II. Present Level of Educational Performance:

Mary has limited vision. She can progress in the regular curriculum with the use of adapted materials (large print materials) and with an adaptation of the performance standard (using high-interest, low vocabulary literature). Mary benefits from cooperative learning groups.

III. Annual Goal:

Mary will be able to read literary materials and identify the characters, the setting, the mood, and the plot of the story. She will be able to apply these literary devices into the development of a short story.

Benchmarks or Short-Term Objectives	Type of Curriculum	Type of Adaptation	Performance Task	Performance Assessment
Mary will name the characters of the story.	Regular Curriculum	Braille Books	Cooperative Learning Groups	Teacher Observation
Mary will be able to describe the main character of the story.	Regular Curriculum	None	Cooperative Learning Group	Teacher Observation
Mary will write a short story and include these literary devices in her story.	Regular Curriculum	Use of Braille keyboard and Braille printer	Typing story	Use of rubric

In addition to being a contributing member of the regular classroom and having the ability to participate in the general curriculum, Mary requires an individual curriculum that teaches the skills of maneuvering around her classroom and the school. These special services are provided by an orientation and mobility specialist. An example of her individual curriculum is shown in Figure 12.3.

Now consider Melissa. Melissa is a moderately mentally disabled student. She is seventeen years of age and is receiving services in a self-contained classroom. She is mainstreamed for art, music, and physical education. Her IEP committee has met and determined that the general curriculum is not appropriate for her. The career goal for Melissa is to transition into a sheltered workshop environment and to live in an assisted community setting. Her special curriculum is shown in Figure 12.4 (Loyd & Brolin, 1997).

FIGURE 12.4. STANDARDS-BASED IEP

Benchmarks or Short-Term Objectives	Type of Curricula	Type of Adaptation	Performance Task	Performance Assessment
Melissa will select a weekly shopping list from a picture menu.	Special Curriculum	Use of pictorial grocery list	Use of pictures to paste a pictorial grocery list	Teacher assessment of grocery list
Melissa will be able to locate food items in the grocery story.	Special Curriculum	Help of teacher assistant	Select item and place in grocery cart	Ability to match pictures from list with items in cart

FIGURE 12.3. STANDARDS-BASED IEP

I. Student: <u>Mary Smith</u>   DOB: <u>11/9/87</u>

School: Grade: From: To:
   <u>Newton Elementary</u>   <u>6</u>   <u>6/2/99</u>   <u>6/1/2000</u>

II. Present Level of Educational Performance:

Mary is able to use a cane to maneuver around her home and yard.

III. Annual Goal:

Mary will be able to use a cane to maneuver around her class-room, down the halls, in the media center, the bathroom, the gym, and the cafeteria.

Benchmarks or Short-Term Objectives	Type of Curriculum	Type of Adaptation	Performance Task	Performance Assessment
Mary will be able to walk assisted down the hall to all the locations required daily for her class schedule.	Individual curriculum	Use of cane and services of orientation and mobility specialist	Walk throughout school building with assistance	Successfully walking with assistance
Mary will be able to walk unassisted down the hall to all the locations required daily for her class schedule.	Individual curriculum	Use of cane	Walk throughout school building unassisted	Successfully walking without assistance

USING THE LONG-TERM PLAN

The long-term plan shows what will be taught over a semester or year. It provides a framework, and at the same time allows for flexibility. The long-term plan for Mary's class would look something similar to that shown in Figure 12.5.

FIGURE 12.5. LONG-TERM PLAN FOR MARY

Week	Events	Unit Title	Source	Standard	Benchmarks
Jan. 1–5	New Year's Holiday	Icabod Crane: Legend of Sleepy Hollow	Regular Curriculum	Use of literary devices	Character, setting, mood
Jan. 8–12		Icabod Crane: Legend of Sleepy Hollow	Regular Curriculum	Use of literary devices	Plot

The regular curriculum is being taught but is modified through the use of adaptive technology for Mary. She is able to achieve the same benchmarks as the other students. For Melissa, the long-term plan would be similar to that shown in Figure 12.6.

FIGURE 12.6. LONG-TERM PLAN FOR MELISSA

Week	Events	Unit Title	Source	Standard	Benchmarks
Jan. 1–5	New Year's Holiday	Eating at Home and in the Community	Special Curriculum	Purchasing Food	Purchasing food in classroom store
Jan. 8–12	Field Trip to Grocery Store	Eating at Home and in the Community	Special Curriculum	Purchasing Food	Purchasing food in grocery store

In developing the long-term plan, it is necessary to review the IEPs of the students in the classroom and consider the goals and benchmarks of each student. This will aid in unit development and will also determine the amount of time that needs to be spent on a particular unit.

USING PERFORMANCE TASKS

A performance task is a complex open-ended problem that the student must solve or master (see Chapter 8). The task must be aligned with the curriculum content (Elliot, 1994). The performance task may be part of the regular curriculum with modifications, as in the case of Mary who must use a Braille processor and Braille printer in order to write her short story. It could also be a task that is specific to one student. Again, Mary, as a visually impaired student, must be able to master the task of getting about the school building unassisted with the use of a cane.

Melissa is an example of a student who has specific tasks that must be completed as a part of her special curriculum. Because of the nature of her curriculum, Melissa must be able to apply her skills in a community setting. Thus, she has to be able to purchase grocery items in a store setting in her classroom as well as completing the performance task of purchasing specific food items in a grocery store.

USING PERFORMANCE ASSESSMENT

A performance assessment is an evaluation of the student's performance in completing a particular task (See Chapter 9). (Others define the term differently: the Division of Innovation and Development in the U.S. Department of Education's Office of Special Education defined performance assessment as requiring the student to create an answer or a product rather than simply filing in a blank, or stating whether a sentence is true or false.) Most experts believe that the performance tasks should be authentic, used in the real world (Elliot, 1994).

In the case of Mary, she is expected not only to define character, setting, mood and plot, but she must be able to applies these literary devices in the writing of her own short story. The

teacher develops a rubric or scoring guide that will define an exemplary story, an adequate story, a minimal story, or an inadequate story (Fuchs, 1994). An example of such a rubric is shown
in Figure 12.7.

FIGURE 12.7. SAMPLE RUBRIC, LITERARY DEVICES

4. Exemplary story
    4.1.   Student is able to write a short story with
            defined characters.
    4.2.   Student is able to develop a short story with
            a well-developed plot.
    4.3.   Student is able to set the tone for the mood
            of the story.
    4.4.   Student is able to define a setting that is ap-
            propriate for the story.
    4.5.   All paragraphs are well developed.
    4.6.   There are no grammatical errors.
3. Adequate story
    3.1.   Student is able to write a short story that in-
            cludes at least three of the literary devices.
    3.2.   Most of the paragraphs are well developed.
    3.3.   There are fewer than 3 grammatical errors.
2. Minimal story
    2.1.   Student is able to write a short story that in-
            cludes at least two of the literary devices.
    2.2.   Some of the paragraphs are well developed.
    2.1.   There are fewer than 5 grammatical errors.
1. Inadequate story
    1.1.   There is no development of any of the 4 lit-
            erary devices.
    1.2.   There are no well-developed paragraphs.
    1.3.   There are at least 8 grammatical errors.

Melissa is expected to be able to shop for grocery items. An example of her rubric is depicted in Figure 12.8.

FIGURE 12.8. SAMPLE RUBRIC, PURCHASING FOOD

---

4. Exemplary Shopping

    4.1.   Student is successful in locating all of the grocery items without assistance.

    4.2.   Student marks off each item on grocery list after locating it.

    4.3.   Student is able to take food selections to cashier and unload grocery cart onto conveyer belt without assistance.

    4.4.   Student is able to pay for food items without assistance.

    4.5.   Student is able to take and load groceries in car.

3. Useful Shopping

    3.1.   Student is successful in locating some of the grocery items without assistance.

    3.2.   Student marks off some items on grocery list after locating them.

    3.3.   Student is able to take food selections to cashier and unload grocery cart onto conveyer belt without assistance.

    3.4.   Student is able to pay for food items with assistance.

    3.5.   Student is able to take and load groceries in car without assistance.

2. Minimal Shopping

    2.1.   Student is successful in locating some of the grocery items without assistance.

    2.2.   Student cannot locate cashier at front of store without assistance.

    2.3.   Student is able to unload grocery cart onto conveyer belt with assistance.

    2.4.   Student is able to pay for food items with assistance.

(Figure continues on next page.)

    2.5.   Student is able to take and load groceries in car with assistance.

1. Inadequate Shopping
    1.1.   Student is unsuccessful in gathering any of the grocery items on the list.
    1.2.   Student does not exhibit appropriate behavior in the grocery store.

USING TEACHING STANDARDS

All students deserve a quality education. This can be insured by making appropriate decisions about the curriculum that is appropriate for the individual learner, whether the student is taught the standard curriculum, the special curriculum, the individual curriculum or a combination thereof. Thus, the IEP is essential for seeing that students with disabilities receive this quality education.

REFERENCES

Elliot, S. N. (1994). *Creating meaningful performance assessments: Fundamental concepts.* Reston, VA: The Council for Exceptional Children.

Fuchs, L. S. (1994). *Connecting performance assessment to instruction.* Reston, VA: The Council for Exceptional Children.

Individuals With Disabilities Education Act, 34 C.F.R. part 300 (1997).

Loyd, R. J., & Brolin, D. E. (1997). *Life centered career education.* Reston, VA: The Council for Exceptional Children.

13

USING LEARNING STRUCTURES THAT MEET THE STANDARDS

The term *learning structures* is used here to denote the way resources are organized and used to facilitate student learning. This chapter focuses on those learning structures that seem to impinge directly on student learning. The structures are summarized in Figure 13.1 (p. 182) and discussed below.

USE APPROPRIATE CURRICULUM STRUCTURE

Curriculum structure refers to the extent to which the curriculum is based on single subject or two or more subjects. Typically the term *integration* is used to describe several types of connectedness. However, the following distinctions are significant.

Unified curriculum refers to combining several components of one subject, rather than presenting those components separately. Thus, a unified science curriculum would not be delivered as the separate components of biology, chemistry, physics, and earth science. Instead it would emphasize the concepts that cut across all those disciplines, organized according to themes or processes of inquiry.

Correlated curricula are two related curricula (such as science and mathematics) that are closely matched in content. Thus, the tenth-grade student taking science uses the mathematics concepts and skills that have been learned in the tenth-grade mathematics class.

Integrated curricula combine the content of two or more subjects, woven around a common theme. For example, a unit on water pollution might include content from social studies, science, and mathematics.

FIGURE 13.1. STRUCTURES AND STANDARDS

The learning of students with disabilities is more likely to be enhanced when the following standards for learning structures are met.

1. Curriculum

   The curriculum is structured so that students with disabilities can see the connections between the various subjects. At the same time, focused instruction is provided for the acquisition of basic skills.

2. Instructors

   Though instruction is provided chiefly by certificated teachers and specialists, instructional power is enhanced by using peers, parents, community volunteers, and teacher aides.

3. Time

   Time is used flexibly to enhance learning. Longer periods of learning are used to slow the pace of learning as needed and to facilitate depth of learning. Shorter blocks of time are used as needed, to foster attentiveness, to provide for practice, and to reinforce learning.

4. Grouping

   Grouping of students with disabilities for instruction is flexible, determined on the basis of students' needs and strengths. Grouping decisions are flexible and open to change. For most learning, heterogeneous grouping is used.

5. Group Size

   Much of the learning takes place in small groups, supplemented by individual instruction when that seems appropriate. Whole-class instruction is used only rarely.

The research tends to support the use of curriculum integration (Vars, 1991). However, critics have cautioned against the dangers of excessive integration. (See Brophy & Alleman, 1991; Roth, 1994; Gardner & Boix-Mansilla, 1994.) They have two concerns: integrated units often slight subject matter knowledge, and many are poorly designed collection of activities. The other concern for teachers of students with disabilities is that most of those students seem to profit from basic skills instruction that derives from separate disciplines—mathematics and English language arts.

The recommendation for teachers is to use a single subject approach in teaching the basic skills and to integrate the curriculum to help students with disabilities solve problems that transcend the separate disciplines.

VARY THE INSTRUCTIONAL SOURCE

In most inclusive learning contexts, instruction will be provided by the classroom teacher in collaboration with the special educator. However, the team should work to increase the instructional resources, using individual tutoring provided by teacher aides, peers, and community volunteers. (See Walberg, 1990; and McGregor & Vogelsberg, 1998.) If noncertificated personnel are used, they should have training in the skills of tutoring. Tutors also need to have an attitude of genuine acceptance of students with disabilities and a desire to help. Note also that some excellent computer programs are available that serve as tutors (Bransford, Brown, & Cocking, 1999).

Tutors provide several advantages in the inclusive classroom. They enable the tutor to work with the students with disabilities on the special and individual curricula. They make it possible to have a one-on-one interaction with the student. They can give immediate feedback when necessary. And they can readily change the teaching approach if the student seems to be having trouble.

USE TIME FLEXIBLY

Students with disabilities learn best when time is used flexibly, instead of serving as the captives of a rigid schedule. Most students with disabilities seem to profit from a slower learning pace. As one teacher observed ironically, "The main characteristic of slow learners is that they learn slowly."

Several means can be used to achieve time flexibility. Elementary teachers in a self-contained classroom can vary time almost at will by simply ending one task and beginning another. Even secondary teachers using the standard 45-minute period can achieve time flexibility by dividing the period into three shorter phases, each focusing on a single stage of learning and a different method, like the one shown in Figure 13.2.

FIGURE 13.2. EXAMPLE OF TIME FLEXIBILITY

Classroom Time	Instructional Purpose	Instructional Method
0–10 minutes	Review; check homework	Oral questions; board work
11–25 minutes	Teach new concept: *soil erosion*	Concept development
26–45 minutes	Students discuss local erosion problem in small groups	Small group discussion

The block schedule, which gives students four 90-minute periods for one term, can also be used flexibly. The only caution is not to increase "teacher-talk" time. Several anecdotal reports suggest that many teachers lecture for 45 minutes and then have students do seat work for 45:

USE GROUPING STRATEGIES FLEXIBLY

The term *grouping* includes several related approaches to the issue of how to group students for learning.

TRACKING

Tracking is assigning students to a single group for most of their instruction, using such labels as *general, vocational, college preparatory, gifted,* and *special.* Thus, students in the vocational track would be together for all their academic subjects, assigned to courses called *vocational English, vocational science,* and *vocational math.*

Several criticisms have been made of curriculum tracking, especially as it affects students in the less prestigious vocational and general tracks.

First, such tracks tend to be dead ends for students who have taken courses that are not accepted by most four-year colleges. Such tracks also prepare students for mastering the specific job-related skills of obsolete vocations, when some evidence suggests that adults change careers several times in a lifetime. Furthermore, the curriculum for the academically less able is second rate; students are not challenged.

Instructional processes for the lower tracked student use primarily teacher-talk and drill and practice. Finally curriculum tracking tends to perpetuate social class bias: most of the poor minority students find themselves in the lower track. (See Oakes & Wells, 1996.) All these criticisms seem to apply to the practice of tracking students with disabilities.

WITHIN-CLASS GROUPING

Most elementary teachers use *within-class grouping.* In this grouping mode, teachers are assigned a heterogeneous class. The teachers then organize reading groups and math groups on the basis of students' ability in those subjects. Some researchers believe that within-class grouping is the best way to teach basic skills. Many teachers who practice inclusive approaches use within-class grouping; they are assigned a heterogeneous class and then group together students with disabilities.

HOMOGENEOUS GROUPING

In homogeneous grouping, school administrators attempt to assign homogeneous groups to teachers in the core academic areas, except in social studies classes where heterogeneity seems to be the pattern. Such grouping decisions are usually made on the bases of previous grades in that subject, scores on standardized tests, and teacher and counselor recommendations. The research generally supports heterogeneous grouping for all students except the gifted.

Though heterogeneity is generally desirable, teachers of students with disabilities should be flexible. The essential question is this one: "What grouping pattern will be best for this particular student with this disability?" Thus, the teacher might begin with a heterogeneous class of 25 students with a wide range of ability, including four students with a mild disability. When the students with disabilities need special instruction in the special curriculum, she brings them together in a cluster group. Then when she wants the class to solve a complex multidisciplinary problem, she assigns one student with a disability to each problem solving group.

USE SMALL GROUP AND INDIVIDUAL INSTRUCTION

This standard suggests that teachers who work with students with disabilities should in general use small groups and individual instruction, minimizing the use of whole class instruction.

SMALL GROUPS

As noted above, small groups can be heterogeneous or homogeneous in nature. If at all possible, teachers should organize the groups so that there are from four to seven students in each group. Once the group gets beyond seven in number, it seems to lose many of the advantages of the small group. Students with disabilities will need to be taught the key skills needed for small group work. The following skills seem to be the most important ones, phrased as suggestions to students that might be posted on the classroom bulletin board for all students:

- Contribute all you can
- Listen closely
- Take turns
- Keep hands to yourself
- Stay on task

Both homogeneous and heterogeneous small groups can accomplish many learning tasks. They can discuss issues. They can use the computer together to play learning games. They can use concrete materials to facilitate learning. The members can teach each other. They can solve problems together. In general, whatever works in a whole class setting will work even better in a small group.

INDIVIDUAL INSTRUCTION

One-on-one teaching has always been part of the repertoire of effective teachers of students with disabilities. Such an approach seems especially needed in inclusive classrooms that include a wide range of academic abilities. The one-on-one instruction, as noted above, might be provided by the teacher, by the special educator, by a human or technological tutor.

Though individual instruction has all the advantages indicated above, it is not always better than small group learning. Much of the learning needed by students with disabilities involves the social learning that the small group can best provide.

WHOLE-CLASS INSTRUCTION

Though the inclusive class will make relatively little use of whole class instruction, it can be useful as a means of creating and sustaining the culture of a learning community. It is in the whole class that the special knowledge and strengths of students with disabilities can best be acknowledged. And it is in whole class teaching/learning activities that the teacher can provide legitimate opportunities for the students with disabilities to gain acceptance by peers.

Teachers with inclusive classes will find that any activity that does not spotlight the students' disabilities can be effective in a whole class environment. The teacher can use several strategies to foster the inclusive learning community in a whole class setting. First, they may ask questions of varying levels of difficulty, as in this exchange.

Teacher: Jorge (student with no disability), can you explain the Bill of Rights?

Student: They are in the first ten amendments. They include freedom of speech, freedom of the press, and some others I have forgotten.

Teacher: Let's take an example of freedom of speech. Maria (student with mild disability), in our country can a person be sent to jail for criticizing the President?

They can also select content and activities that do not require skills that student with disabilities lack. For example, a whole class studying World War II might view a videotape of some of the key battles and then discuss how that war differed from the Gulf War. A student with a learning disability could profit from both the viewing and the discussion—and can contribute if the right kind of question is asked.

A CONCLUDING NOTE

Although the recommended structures are well grounded in research, they must be used with care and flexibility. Each student with a disability is a unique individual, whose learning needs probably differ significantly from those of the rest of the group. The availability of resources also varies from school to school. Therefore, the best advice is to assess the students needs and provide whatever structure will lead to better learning.

REFERENCES

Bransford, J. D., Brown, A. L., & Cocking, R. R. (1999). *How people learn*. Washington, DC: National Academy Press.

Brophy, J., & Alleman, J. (1991). A caveat: Curriculum integration isn't always a good idea. *Educational Leadership, 49* (2), 66.

Gardner, H., & Boix-Mansilla, V. (1994). Teaching for understanding in the disciplines—and beyond. *Teachers College Record, 96,* 198–218.

McGregor, G., & Vogelsberg, R. T. (1998). *Inclusive schooling practices: Pedagogical and research foundations.* Baltimore: Brookes.

Oakes, J., & Wells, A. (1996). *Beyond the technicalities of school reform.* Los Angeles: UCLA Graduate School of Education and Information Studies.

Roth, K. J. (1994). Second thoughts about interdisciplinary studies. *American Educator, 18* (1), 44–48.

Vars, G. F. (1991). Integrated curriculum in historical perspective. *Educational Leadership, 49* (2), 14–15.

Walberg, H. J. (1990). Productive teaching and instruction: The knowledge base. *Phi Delta Kappan, 72,* 470–478.